Mini PRAYERS *that* PREVAIL

Written and Compiled by

CLIFT RICHARDS

——— *with* ———

LLOYD HILDEBRAND

Victory House, Inc.
Tulsa, Oklahoma

MINI PRAYERS THAT PREVAIL
Copyright © 1996 by K & C International, Inc.
ISBN: 0-932081-35-5
Printed in the United States of America

Published by Victory House, Inc.
P.O. Box 700238
Tulsa, Oklahoma 74170
(918) 747-5009

Cover Design by: *Whitley Graphics*

OTHER BOOKS OF INTEREST

A Little Bit of God's Wisdom and Wit
A Little Bit of God's Wisdom and Wit for Men
A Little Bit of God's Wisdom and Wit for Women
Prayers That Prevail — The Believer's Manual of Prayers
More Prayers That Prevail
Prayers That Prevail for America — Changing a Nation Through Prayer
Prayers That Prevail for Your Children — A Parent's and Grandparent's
      Manual of Prayers
Mini Prayers That Prevail
God's Special Promises to Me

All titles are available at your local
bookstore or through Victory House, Inc.

INTRODUCTION

Therefore I say to you, whatever things you ask when you pray, believe that you receive them, and you will have them.
(Mark 11:24, NKJV)

It has often been said that, "Good things come in little packages." This expression has never been more true than it is in the case of the little book you hold in your hands. Like the four larger books in the very popular *Prayers That Prevail* series, *Mini Prayers That Prevail* is filled with powerful topical prayers that are built directly from God's Word.

As you incorporate these God-breathed, promise-packed prayers into your daily life, you will discover that the Father has much more in store for you than you ever imagined.

The prayers themselves relate to your daily concerns, including Christian growth, interpersonal relationships, spiritual warfare, applying the principles of faith, and personal happiness. As you use this little book, the windows of heaven will open unto you and you will see that your heavenly Father is truly able "...to do exceedingly abundantly above all that we ask or think, according to the power that works in us" (Eph. 3:20, NKJV).

• ABIDING IN CHRIST •

Key Scripture: "I am the vine, you are the branches. He who abides in Me, and I in him, bears much fruit; for without Me you can do nothing" (John 15:5, NKJV).

Prayer: Father God, you are the vinedresser.[1] Cultivate and prune my life so that I will bear more fruit.[2] Thank you for cleansing me through your Word.[3] I will abide in the True Vine, your Son, my Savior, Jesus Christ.[4] As I abide in Him, and let your Word abide in me, I will definitely receive answers to my prayers.[5] Thank you for this wonderful prayer promise. In Jesus' name I pray,[6] Amen.

References: (1) John 15:1; (2) John 15:2; (3) John 15:3; (4) John 15:4; (5) John 15:7; (6) John 16:23.

• ABUNDANT LIFE •

Key Scripture: "The thief does not come except to steal, and to kill, and to destroy. I have come that they may have life, and that they may have it more abundantly" (John 10:10, NKJV).

Prayer: Lord God,[1] thank you for abundant life.[2] You are the God of abundant grace and love.[3] Thank you for supplying all my needs according to your riches in glory through Christ Jesus.[4] I will walk in the abundant joy,[5] mercy,[6] and grace[7] you provide. I will continue to trust you with all my heart, never leaning to my own understanding; in all my ways I will acknowledge you, and I know you will direct my paths.[8] This is the key to abundant living. In Jesus' name I pray,[9] Amen.

References: (1) Ezekiel 5:5; (2) John 10:10; (3) 1 Timothy 1:14; (4) Philippians 4:19; (5) 2 Corinthians 8:2; (6) Hebrews 4:16; (7) 2 Corinthians 4:15; (8) Proverbs 3:5-6; (9) John 16:24.

• AGREEMENT •

Key Scripture: "Again I say to you that if two of you agree on earth concerning anything that they ask, it will be done for them by My Father in heaven" (Matt. 18:19, NKJV).

Prayer: Loving Father,[1] thank you for the power of agreement.[2] When I gather with other believers, and pray, you are present with us.[3] You assure me that whatever we bind on earth shall be bound in heaven, and whatever we loose on earth will be loosed in heaven.[4] I will walk in agreement with you,[5] your Word,[6] your will,[7] and my fellow-believers.[8] In Jesus' name I pray,[9] Amen.

References: (1) Matthew 18:10; (2) Matthew 18:18-19; (3) Matthew 18:20; (4) Matthew 18:18; (5) 2 Corinthians 6:16; (6) John 17:17; (7) 1 John 5:14-15; (8) John 17:21; (9) John 16:23.

• ANGELS •

Key Scripture: "For he will command his angels concerning you to guard you in all your ways" (Ps. 91:11, NIV).

Prayer: Father in heaven,[1] thank you for the angelic host who carry your messages,[2] protect me,[3] minister to me,[4] and watch over me.[5] In your heavenly realm there are thousands of chariots and tens of thousands of angels.[6] These wonderful messengers excel in strength, do your commandments, and hearken to do your Word.[7] Lord, it is so comforting to me to realize that these heavenly beings encamp around me and deliver me.[8] Thank you for their constant care and protection. Through the name of Christ, my Lord,[9] Amen.

References: (1) Isaiah 64:8; (2) Psalms 103:20; (3) Psalms 34:7; (4) Hebrews 1:7; (5) Psalms 91:11-12; (6) Psalms 68:17; (7) Psalms 103:20; (8) Psalms 34:7; (9) John 15:16.

• ANGER •

Key Scripture: "But now you must rid yourselves of all such things as these: anger, rage, malice, slander, and filthy language from your lips" (Col. 3:8, NIV).

Prayer: Gracious Lord,[1] you are always ready to pardon, merciful, slow to anger, and of great kindness.[2] I want to be like you, to be conformed to the image of your Son,[3] my Lord and Savior, Jesus Christ.[4] With your help, I will remove all bitterness, wrath, anger, and evil speaking from my life.[5] I never want to grieve your Spirit through inappropriate anger, Lord,[6] and so I ask you to fill me with your grace so that I will always be tender-hearted as you have been with me.[7] In Jesus' name I pray,[8] Amen.

References: (1) Psalms 33:22; (2) Nehemiah 9:17; (3) 2 Corinthians 3:18; (4) 1 Thessalonians 5:9; (5) Ephesians 4:31; (6) Ephesians 4:30; (7) Ephesians 4:32; (8) John 16:23.

God looks for people who trust Him fully; in them He will show His power

(Andrew Murray).

Trust in the Lord with all thine heart; and lean not unto thine own understanding. In all thy ways acknowledge him, and he shall direct thy paths (Proverbs 3:5-6).

• ANOINTING •

Key Scripture: "But the anointing which you have received from Him abides in you, ...and just as it has taught you, you will abide in Him" (1 John 2:27, NKJV).

Prayer: Father of glory,[1] thank you for the anointing I have received through Jesus Christ.[2] He was anointed to preach the Gospel, to set the captives free, to give sight to the blind, and to heal the broken-hearted.[3] Because He lives within me,[4] I know that I can walk in His anointing as well.[5] Thank you for anointing me with gladness,[6] power,[7] and love.[8] Your anointing in my life has destroyed every yoke of bondage.[9] In the name of Jesus Christ,[10] Amen.

References: (1) Ephesians 1:17; (2) 1 John 2:27; (3) Luke 4:18; (4) Colossians 1:27; (5) 2 Corinthians 1:21; (6) Hebrews 1:9; (7) Acts 1:8; (8) 1 Corinthians 13; (9) Isaiah 10:27; (10) John 15:16.

The beginning of anxiety is the end of faith, and the beginning of true faith is the end of anxiety

(George Muller).

The just shall live by faith (Romans 1:17).

• ANXIETY •

Key Scripture: "Do not be anxious about anything, but in everything, by prayer and petition, with thanksgiving, present your requests to God. And the peace of God, which transcends all understanding, will guard your hearts and your minds in Christ Jesus" (Phil. 4:6-7, NIV).

Prayer: Loving Lord,[1] thank you for the peace you provide to lift me out of all anxiety.[2] Your peace guards my heart and mind.[3] You keep me in perfect peace as I place all my trust in you.[4] Because I know you care about me, I am able to cast all my anxiety upon you.[5] Anxiety is really fear of the future, and I thank you that your perfect loves casts all the fear and anxiety out of my life.[6] Thank you, Father. In Jesus' name I pray,[7] Amen.

References: (1) Psalms 87:2; (2) Philippians 4:7; (3) Philippians 4:7; (4) Isaiah 26:3; (5) 1 Peter 5:7; (6) 1 John 4:18; (7) John 16:23.

• ASSURANCE •

Key Scripture: "I write these things to you who believe in the name of the Son of God so that you may know that you have eternal life" (1 John 5:13, NIV).

Prayer: Almighty God,[1] thank you for the assurance of eternal life that you give to all who love you.[2] Because I confess Jesus Christ as my Lord, and I believe in my heart that you raised Him from the dead, I have eternal life.[3] I have been born again.[4] I am a new creation in Christ Jesus.[5] Your wonderful promise assures me that those who come to you will never be cast out.[6] In Jesus' name,[7] Amen.

References: (1) Genesis 17:1; (2) John 3:16; (3) Romans 10:9; (4) John 3:7; (5) 2 Corinthians 5:17; (6) John 6:37; (7) John 15:16.

• ATTITUDES •

Key Scripture: "Finally, brothers, whatever is true, whatever is noble, whatever is right, whatever is pure, whatever is lovely, whatever is admirable — if anything is excellent or praiseworthy — think about such things" (Phil. 4:8, NIV).

Prayer: Lord of lords,[1] your Word renews the attitudes of my heart and mind.[2] Your way is perfect,[3] and you keep me in perfect peace when I keep my mind stayed on you.[4] Thank you for the peace that surpasses all understanding that you have given so freely to me.[5] It truly guards my heart and mind.[6] Father, I will let the Beatitudes of Jesus be the attitudes of my heart.[7] Help me to walk in integrity at all times.[8] These things I pray in Jesus' name,[9] Amen.

References: (1) Revelation 19:16; (2) Ephesians 4:23; (3) Psalms 18:30; (4) Isaiah 26:3; (5) Philippians 4:7; (6) Philippians 4:7; (7) Matthew 5:1-12; (8) Proverbs 11:3; (9) John 16:23.

Never, never, never, never give up.

Therefore put on the full armor of God, so that when the day of evil comes, you may be able to stand your ground, and after you have done everything, to stand (Ephesians 6:13, NIV).

• AUTHORITY •

Key Scripture: "Behold, I give you the authority to trample on serpents and scorpions, and over all the power of the enemy, and nothing shall by any means hurt you" (Luke 10:19, NKJV).

Prayer: O Lord,[1] I thank you for the spiritual authority you have imparted to me through prayer,[2] your Word,[3] the blood of Jesus,[4] the indwelling Holy Spirit,[5] and the name of Jesus Christ.[6] You have given me authority over all the power of the enemy; therefore I realize that nothing shall by any means hurt me.[7] I know that I can do all things through Christ who strengthens me.[8] Strengthen me with might by your Spirit in my inner man now as I pray,[9] in the mighty name of Jesus,[10] Amen.

References: (1) Psalms 143:11; (2) John 14:13; (3) Ephesians 6:17; (4) Revelation 12:11; (5) Romans 8:11; (6) Mark 16:17; (7) Luke 10:19; (8) Philippians 4:13; (9) Ephesians 3:16; (10) John 15:16.

Faith is not a sense, nor sight, nor reason, but taking God at His Word.

(Arthur Benoni Evans)

For we walk by faith, not by sight (2 Corinthians 5:7).

• THE BIBLE •

Key Scripture: "Your word is a lamp to my feet and a light for my path" (Ps. 119:105, NIV).

Prayer: Eternal God,[1] thank you for your Word. It keeps me from sin.[2] It renews my mind.[3] It sanctifies me.[4] I will let your Word dwell in me richly in all wisdom.[5] I will preach your Word,[6] because I know you have inspired your Word; it is my source for doctrine, reproof, correction, and instruction in righteousness.[7] Through your Word I will become complete, fully prepared to do good works in your name.[8] Through Christ, the living Word,[9] I pray, Amen.

References: (1) Deuteronomy 33:27; (2) Psalms 119:11; (3) Ephesians 4:23; (4) Ephesians 5:26; (5) Colossians 3:16; (6) 2 Timothy 4:2; (7) 2 Timothy 3:16; (8) 2 Timothy 3:17; (9) John 1:1.

Become better, not bitter.

Looking diligently lest any man fail of the grace of God; lest any root of bitterness springing up trouble you, and thereby many be defiled (Hebrews 12:15).

• BITTERNESS •

Key Scripture: "See to it that no one misses the grace of God and that no bitter root grows up to cause trouble and defile many" (Heb. 12:15, NIV).

Prayer: King of kings,[1] I come before your throne with confidence, knowing that I will receive mercy and grace to help in my time of need.[2] With your help, I will remove all bitterness, wrath, anger, and evil speaking from my life.[3] I will replace those negative attributes with kindness and tender-heartedness. I will walk in forgiveness, Father, even as you have forgiven me for Christ's sake.[4] I will walk in love in the same way that Christ has loved me.[5] Thank you for giving me the oil of gladness in place of the gall of bitterness.[6] In Jesus' name I pray,[7] Amen.

References: (1) Revelation 19:16; (2) Hebrews 4:16; (3) Ephesians 4:31; (4) Ephesians 4:32; (5) Ephesians 5:2; (6) Hebrews 1:9; (7) John 15:16.

• BLESSEDNESS •

Key Scripture: "Now then, my sons, listen to me; blessed are those who keep my ways. Listen to my instruction and be wise....For whoever finds me finds life and receives favor from the Lord" (Prov. 8:33-35, NIV).

Prayer: Lord of lords,[1] your bountiful blessings in my life make me truly happy.[2] You have blessed me with all spiritual blessings in heavenly places in Christ.[3] I walk in blessedness because I have placed my trust in you.[4] The teachings of your Word enable me to walk in the blessedness you have provided for me.[5] Thank you for blessing my life so richly, Father.[6] In the name of the Lord I pray,[7] Amen.

References: (1) Revelation 19:16; (2) Proverbs 28:20; (3) Ephesians 1:3; (4) Psalms 2:12; (5) Psalms 94:12; (6) Proverbs 10:22; (7) John 12:13.

• THE BLOOD OF JESUS •

Key Scripture: "In him we have redemption through his blood, the forgiveness of sins, in accordance with the riches of God's grace" (Eph. 1:7, NIV).

Prayer: Loving God,[1] your covenant with me required that Jesus' blood be shed for the atonement of my sins.[2] I am now justified by His blood.[3] My sins are forgiven.[4] My future is secure.[5] I have access to you, Father,[6] and spiritual victory.[7] My fear is gone,[8] and I know you are near to me.[9] I thank you for the precious blood of Christ.[10] In Jesus' name I pray,[11] Amen.

References: (1) John 16:27; (2) Leviticus 17:11; (3) Romans 5:9; (4) Hebrews 9:22; (5) Romans 5:9; (6) Ephesians 2:18; (7) Revelation 12:11; (8) Exodus 12:13; (9) Psalms 46:1; (10) Romans 5:8; (11) John 15:16.

• BOLDNESS •

Key Scripture: "According to the eternal purpose which He accomplished in Christ Jesus our Lord, in whom we have boldness and access with confidence through faith in Him" (Eph. 3:11, NKJV).

Prayer: Heavenly Father,[1] your grace permits me to come boldly before your throne in order to obtain mercy and find grace to help me in my times of need.[2] Faith in your Word enables me to be as bold as a lion.[3] I will speak boldly in your behalf,[4] Lord, as I hold forth your Word of Life to the people I meet.[5] Thank you for giving me great boldness through faith in Jesus Christ.[6] I will never be ashamed to share Him with others.[7] In Jesus' name I pray,[8] Amen.

References: (1) Luke 11:2; (2) Hebrews 4:16; (3) Proverbs 28:1; (4) Ephesians 6:20; (5) Philippians 2:16; (6) 1 Timothy 3:13; (7) Romans 1:16; (8) John 15:16.

• BROKENNESS •

Key Scripture: "The sacrifices of God are a broken spirit, A broken and a contrite heart; These, O God, You will not despise" (Ps. 51:17, NKJV).

Prayer: Everlasting Father,[1] revive my spirit and my heart as I humble myself before you.[2] I tremble before your majesty and before the power of your glory and your Word.[3] As I humble myself under your mighty hand, dear Lord, I know I will be exalted in due time.[4] Thank you for being near to me in my time of brokenness.[5] Thank you for your wonderful promises;[6] I will walk in brokenness and humility which will lead me to riches, honor, and life.[7] In Jesus' name I pray,[8] Amen.

References: (1) Luke 11:2; (2) Isaiah 11:2; (3) Isaiah 66:5; (4) 1 Peter 5:6; (5) Psalms 34:18; (6) 2 Peter 1:4; (7) Proverbs 22:4; (8) John 16:23.

Many people mistake our work for our vocation. Our vocation is the love of Jesus.

(Mother Teresa)

He that loveth me not keepeth not my sayings
(John 14:24).

• CALLING •

Key Scripture: "Therefore, brethren, be even more diligent to make your call and election sure, for if you do these things you will never stumble" (2 Peter 1:10, NKJV).

Prayer: Abba, Father,[1] thank you for calling me[2] and choosing me.[3] I will abide in the calling you have put upon my life.[4] I will bear much fruit.[5] You have called me to be both your servant and your free man.[6] Thank you, Father. Enlighten the eyes of my understanding, Lord, so I will know the hope of your calling in my life, and the riches you have given to me.[7] I will always press toward the mark for the prize of your high calling in Christ Jesus.[8] In His name I pray,[9] Amen.

References: (1) Mark 14:36; (2) Romans 11:29; (3) John 15:16; (4) 1 Corinthians 7:20; (5) John 15:16; (6) 1 Corinthians 7:22; (7) Ephesians 1:18; (8) Philippians 3:14; (9) Acts 19:17.

Before you go to bed, turn your worries over to God. He'll be up all night.

He who watches over you will not slumber.
(Psalm 121:3, NIV)

• GOD CARES •

Key Scripture: "Casting all your care on Him, for He cares for you" (1 Peter 5:7, NKJV).

Prayer: Father,[1] thank you for caring about me.[2] You do not want me to be anxious or fearful about anything;[3] therefore, I cast all of my cares — anxieties, worries, and fears — on you.[4] You are my shepherd,[5] guide,[6] healer,[7] and deliverer.[8] I receive your care, Father, because I know you love and understand me.[9] In Jesus' name,[10] Amen.

References: (1) Luke 11:2; (2) 1 Peter 5:7; (3) Philippians 4:6; (4) 1 Peter 5:7; (5) Psalms 23:1; (6) Psalms 32:8; (7) Exodus 15:26; (8) Psalms 37:40; (9) Psalms 139:2; (10) John 16:24.

What you do in secret reveals the content of your character.

Who can understand his errors? cleanse thou me from secret faults (Psalm 19:12).

• CHARACTER •

Key Scripture: "His divine power has given us everything we need for life and godliness through our knowledge of him who called us by his own glory and goodness" (2 Peter 1:3, NIV).

Prayer: Mighty God,[1] I believe your Word.[2] It is building character in my life as I let its truth dwell in me richly in all wisdom.[3] I will walk in the integrity of my heart[4] which comes from believing and obeying your Word.[5] With your help, Father, I will do everything in the name of my Lord Jesus, giving thanks to you through Him.[6] I will fulfill my responsibilities with the godly character you have imparted to me, working heartily as unto you.[7] In Jesus' name I pray,[8] Amen.

References: (1) Isaiah 9:6; (2) Titus 1:9; (3) Colossians 3:16; (4) Psalms 26:11; (5) Psalms 119:11; (6) Colossians 3:17; (7) Colossians 3:23; (8) Acts 19:17.

• COMFORT •

Key Scripture: "Blessed be the God and Father of our Lord Jesus Christ, the Father of mercies and God of all comfort" (2 Cor. 1:3-4, NKJV).

Prayer: Father of mercies and God of all comfort,[1] thank you for comforting me in the same way a mother comforts her child.[2] I receive the comfort of your Holy Spirit, who is the Comforter, in my life right now.[3] Things that I used to consider gain for me I now willingly give up for Christ.[4] Because of your comfort in my life I now am able to count all things but loss for the excellency of the knowledge of Christ Jesus my Lord, for whom I have suffered the loss of all things so that I may win Him.[5] Thank you, Father. In the name of Jesus,[6] Amen.

References: (1) 2 Corinthians 1:3; (2) Isaiah 66:13; (3) John 14:16-18; (4) Philippians 3:7; (5) Philippians 3:8; (6) 1 Corinthians 1:2.

• COMMITMENT •

Key Scripture: "Nevertheless I am not ashamed: for I know whom I have believed, and am persuaded that he is able to keep that which I have committed unto him against that day" (2 Tim. 1:12).

Prayer: Wonderful Lord,[1] I live and move and have my being in you.[2] I have committed my life to you, and I will continue to hold fast to your Word through the faith and love I have in Christ Jesus.[3] Through your grace I will be strong.[4] Thank you for helping me to keep the commitments I have made to you.[5] I will never be ashamed of the Gospel of Jesus Christ, because I know it is your power unto salvation to everyone that believes.[6] In Jesus' name I pray,[7] Amen.

References: (1) Deuteronomy 30:5; (2) Acts 17:28; (3) 2 Timothy 1:13; (4) 2 Timothy 2:1; (5) 2 Timothy 1:12; (6) Romans 1:16; (7) Acts 9:29.

• COMPASSION •

Key Scripture: "Finally, all of you be of one mind, having compassion for one another; love as brothers, be tenderhearted, be courteous; not returning evil for evil or reviling for reviling, but on the contrary blessing, knowing that you were called to this, that you may inherit a blessing" (1 Peter 3:8-9, NKJV).

Prayer: Father of lights, with whom there is no shadow of turning,[1] thank you for having compassion on me.[2] You always show mercy,[3] and I know you understand everything about me.[4] Through your grace, I will extend compassion to others with love and courtesy, because I know you have called me to be compassionate toward others.[5] Thank you for the blessings I receive when I am compassionate toward other people.[6] In Jesus' name I pray,[7] Amen.

References: (1) James 1:17; (2) Romans 9:15; (3) Romans 9:16; (4) Hebrews 4:15; (5) 1 Peter 3:8-9; (6) 1 Peter 3:9; (7) John 15:16.

• COMPLAINING •

Key Scripture: "And when the people complained it displeased the Lord: and the Lord heard it; and his anger was kindled" (Num.11:1).

Prayer: Lord,[1] your Word shows me that you dislike complaining.[2] I want to please you at all times,[3] and I never want to displease you or make you angry because of complaining.[4] Teach me your ways so that I will always walk in your paths.[5] Realizing that complaining leads to heaviness, negativity, bitterness, and death,[6] I choose to be a positive believer who praises you,[7] speaks your truth in love,[8] and focuses on the things that lead to godliness in my life.[9] In Jesus' name I pray,[10] Amen.

References: (1) Numbers 11:16; (2) Numbers 11:1; (3) Proverbs 16:7; (4) Numbers 11:1; (5) Psalms 27:11; (6) Job 7:11; (7) Psalms 149:1; (8) Ephesians 4:15; (9) 1 Timothy 6:11; (10) Philippians 2:9.

You may trust the Lord too little, but you can never trust Him too much

(Anonymous).

Trust in the Lord with all thine heart; and lean not unto thine own understanding. In all thy ways acknowledge him, and he shall direct thy paths (Proverbs 3:5-6).

• CONDEMNATION •

Key Scripture: "There is therefore now no condemnation to those who are in Christ Jesus, who do not walk according to the flesh, but according to the Spirit. For the law of the Spirit of life in Christ Jesus has made me free from the law of sin and death" (Rom. 8:1-2, NKJV).

Prayer: Lord God,[1] you commended your love toward me in that while I was yet a sinner, Christ Jesus died for me.[2] I have fallen short of your mark many times, but your great gift to me is eternal life.[3] Thank you, Father, for setting me free from sin, death, and all condemnation.[4] I will stand fast in the liberty by which you have set me free,[5] and I will never again accept condemnation in any form in my life.[6] In Jesus' name I pray,[7] Amen.

References: (1) Joshua 10:42; (2) Romans 5:8; (3) Romans 6:23; (4) Romans 8:2; (5) Galatians 5:1; (6) 1 John 3:21; (7) John 16:23.

• CONFIDENCE •

Key Scripture: "This is the confidence we have in approaching God: that if we ask anything according to his will, he hears us. And if we know that he hears us — whatever we ask — we know that we have what we asked of him" (1 John 5:14-15, NIV).

Prayer: Lord, my God,[1] I have great confidence in you[2] because of your great faithfulness in my life.[3] All I have ever needed, your hands have provided for me, and all I will ever need, you will provide for me.[4] Thank you, Father, for the confidence you have imparted to me through your Word that assures me that nothing is impossible with you.[5] In you, O Lord, I place my complete and unswerving trust.[6] In the name of Jesus Christ, my Savior,[7] Amen.

References: (1) Deuteronomy 4:5; (2) Hebrews 10:35; (3) Hebrews 10:23; (4) Philippians 4:19; (5) Matthew 19:26; (6) Psalms 71:1; (7) Titus 3:6.

• CONSISTENCY •

Key Scripture: "Therefore, my beloved brethren, be steadfast, immovable, always abounding in the work of the Lord, knowing that your labor is not in vain in the Lord" (1 Cor. 15:58, NKJV).

Prayer: O Father, Lord of heaven,[1] I choose to be single-minded in my devotion to you because I know that a person who is double-minded is unstable in all his/her ways.[2] Through your Word, I will walk consistently before you because I know you have promised to help me hold my confidence in you steadfastly to the end.[3] As I have received Christ Jesus as my Lord, I want to walk consistently in Him and with Him, rooted and built up in Him and established in the faith as I have been taught.[4] Through Jesus Christ,[5] Amen.

References: (1) Matthew 11:25; (2) James 1:6-8; (3) Hebrews 3:14; (4) Colossians 2:5-9; (5) Romans 1:8.

• CONTENTMENT •

Key Scripture: "Now godliness with contentment is great gain. For we brought nothing into this world, and it is certain we can carry nothing out" (1 Tim. 6:6-7, NKJV).

Prayer: God of peace,[1] thank you for the peace that surpasses all understanding,[2] for rest,[3] and for contentment.[4] I will walk with you in these qualities throughout my life because I know that godliness with contentment is great gain for me.[5] Help me to be like the Apostle Paul by learning to be content regardless of the circumstances,[6] because I know your grace is sufficient for me.[7] Thank you, Father. In Jesus' name,[8] Amen.

References: (1) Romans 15:33; (2) Philippians 4:7; (3) Hebrews 4:11; (4) 1 Timothy 6:8; (5) 1 Timothy 6:6-7; (6) Philippians 4:11; (7) 2 Corinthians 12:9; (8) Acts 4:10.

• COURAGE •

Key Scripture: "Oh, love the Lord, all you His saints! For the Lord preserves the faithful, And fully repays the proud person. Be of good courage, And He shall strengthen your heart, All you who hope in the Lord" (Ps. 31:23-24, NKJV).

Prayer: Dear God almighty,[1] thank you for giving me the courage to be strong.[2] You empower me to be swifter than an eagle and stronger than a lion.[3] Because you are with me, I am strengthened to be a mighty servant of valor like Gideon was.[4] I take my stand upon your promises, Father. I will be strong in you and in the power of your might.[5] As your Spirit gives me power, I will stand courageous; I will not be afraid and I will not be dismayed.[6] Thank you for courage, Lord. In Jesus' name I pray,[7] Amen.

References: (1) Genesis 48:3; (2) 1 Samuel 4:9; (3) 2 Samuel 1:23; (4) Judges 6:12; (5) Ephesians 6:10; (6) 2 Chronicles 32:7; (7) John 16:23.

• COVENANT •

Key Scripture: "He remembers his covenant forever, the word he commanded, for a thousand generations, the covenant he made with Abraham, the oath he swore to Isaac. He confirmed it to Jacob as a decree, to Israel as an everlasting covenant" (Ps. 105:8-10, NIV).

Prayer: God of Abraham, Isaac, and Jacob,[1] I trust you[2] because I know you are faithful to every word of your covenant.[3] Your Word will never return unto you void.[4] The grass withers and the flowers fall, but your Word stands forever.[5] As a covenant person, all my needs are met, according to your glorious riches in Christ Jesus.[6] Thank you, Father. In Jesus' name I pray,[7] Amen.

References: (1) Exodus 3:16; (2) Proverbs 3:5-6; (3) Lamentations 3:23; (4) Isaiah 55:11; (5) Isaiah 40:8; (6) Philippians 4:19; (7) Acts 2:21.

• DEATH •

Key Scripture: "Death is swallowed up in victory....thanks be to God, who gives us the victory through our Lord Jesus Christ" (1 Cor. 15:54-57, NKJV).

Prayer: O Lord,[1] your Son, my Lord and Savior, Jesus Christ, has abolished death. He has brought life and immortality to light through the Gospel.[2] Thank you, Father. I know that I have passed from death into life because I love my brothers and sisters in Christ.[3] If I walk through the valley of the shadow of death, I will fear no evil, for I know you are with me.[4] Goodness and mercy will follow me all the days of my life, and I will dwell in your house forever.[5] In Jesus' name I pray,[6] Amen.

References: (1) Luke 5:8; (2) 2 Timothy 1:10; (3) 1 John 3:14; (4) Psalms 23:4; (5) Psalms 23:6; (6) Acts 4:30.

• DECEPTION •

Key Scripture: "Do not deceive yourselves. If any one of you thinks he is wise by the standards of this age, he should become a 'fool' so that he may become wise. For the wisdom of this world is foolishness in God's sight" (1 Cor. 3:18-19, NIV).

Prayer: Dear Father, you are the only wise God.[1] I pray for your wisdom[2] so that I will never be deceived by myself[3] or anyone else.[4] I ask for your wisdom in faith, nothing wavering, and I know you will impart it to me.[5] Thank you, Father. Help me so that I will let no one deceive me with vain words,[6] or by any other means.[7] Through your grace, I will walk in truth,[8] and your truth will make me free from all deception.[9] In Jesus' name,[10] Amen.

References: (1) Romans 16:27; (2) Proverbs 2:6; (3) 1 John 1:8; (4) Ephesians 5:6; (5) James 1:6; (6) Ephesians 5:6; (7) 2 Thessalonians 2:3; (8) 1 Thessalonians 4:12; (9) John 8:32; (10) John 16:24.

• DELIGHT •

Key Scripture: "Delight yourself also in the Lord, And He shall give you the desires of your heart. Commit your way to the Lord, Trust also in Him, And He shall bring it to pass" (Ps. 37:4-5, NKJV).

Prayer: O Lord, your law is my delight.[1] I take my delight in your Word, and I will meditate upon your Word both day and night.[2] I delight myself in you, Lord.[3] I delight to do your will.[4] I take delight in approaching you, Father.[5] As I take my delight in you, I become more fully aware of the fact that you delight in me.[6] Thank you, Lord. With renewed delight I pray,[7] Amen.

References: (1) Psalms 119:174; (2) Psalms 1:2; (3) Psalms 37:4; (4) Psalms 40:8; (5) Isaiah 58:2; (6) Proverbs 11:20; (7) Psalms 119:16.

• DEPRESSION •

Key Scripture: "Why are you downcast, O my soul? Why so disturbed within me? Put your hope in God, for I will yet praise him, my Savior and my God" (Ps. 43:5, NIV).

Prayer: God, my Rock,[1] you are my joy and my delight, and I will praise you.[2] As the deer pants for streams of living water, so my soul pants for you, O God.[3] My soul thirsts for you, O God, because I know you are the living God.[4] Though my tears have been my food both day and night,[5] I will respond to your love through prayer.[6] I place my hope in you, Father, and I will praise you because you are my Savior and my God.[7] In Jesus' name I pray,[8] Amen.

References: (1) Psalms 42:9; (2) Psalms 43:4; (3) Psalms 42:1; (4) Psalms 42:2; (5) Psalms 42:3; (6) Psalms 42:8; (7) Psalms 42:11; (8) Luke 1:31.

• DILIGENCE •

Key Scripture: "Keep your heart with all diligence, For out of it spring the issues of life" (Prov. 4:23, NKJV).

Prayer: Living God,[1] I thank you that you put riches into the hands of the diligent.[2] Realizing that the hand of the diligent will rule, I determine to walk in diligence before you, Father.[3] Thank you for the precious substance,[4] prosperity,[5] and abundance[6] you give to the diligent. With your help, Father, I will be diligent in my walk with Jesus, so that He will find me to be without spot and blameless when He comes again.[7] In His name I pray,[8] Amen.

References: (1) Psalms 42:2; (2) Proverbs 10:4; (3) Proverbs 12:24; (4) Proverbs 12:27; (5) Proverbs 13:4; (6) Proverbs 21:5; (7) 2 Peter 3:14; (8) John 16:23.

If a door slams shut look for the one God is opening for you.

For I know the plans I have for you, declares the Lord.
(Jeremiah 29:11, NIV)

• DIRECTION •

Key Scripture: "A man's heart plans his way, But the Lord directs his steps" (Prov. 16:9, NKJV).

Prayer: Heavenly Father,[1] thank you for directing my steps.[2] You are my Shepherd, and you lead me in the paths of righteousness for your name's sake.[3] You lead me beside the still waters.[4] I will trust in you, Lord, with all my heart, not leaning unto my own understanding.[5] In all my ways I will acknowledge you, and I know you will direct my paths.[6] I ask you, Father, to direct my heart into a full understanding of your love for me as I patiently wait for the appearing of Jesus Christ.[7] In whose name I pray,[8] Amen.

References: (1) 1 John 1:3; (2) Proverbs 16:9; (3) Psalms 23:3; (4) Psalms 23:2; (5) Proverbs 3:5; (6) Proverbs 3:6; (7) 2 Thessalonians 3:5; (8) John 15:16.

• DISTRESS •

Key Scripture: "In my distress I called upon the Lord, And cried out to my God; He heard my voice from His temple, And my cry came before Him, even to His ears" (Ps. 18:6, NKJV).

Prayer: O Lord,[1] whenever I am in distress and I call upon you, you always hear me.[2] Thank you, Father. You are the God of my righteousness, and you hear me when I cry out to you.[3] You deliver me out of all distress.[4] I praise you and thank you for the certain knowledge that nothing shall ever separate me from your love which I find in Christ Jesus, my Lord.[5] It brings me great joy to realize that all things work together for good in my life because I love you and you have called me.[6] In Jesus' name,[7] Amen.

References: (1) Psalms 18:15; (2) Psalms 120:1; (3) Psalms 4:1; (4) Psalms 107:6; (5) Romans 8:38-39; (6) Romans 8:28; (7) John 16:23.

• ENCOURAGEMENT •

Key Scripture: "And David was greatly distressed; for the people spake of stoning him,...but David encouraged himself in the Lord his God" (1 Sam. 30:6).

Prayer: Heavenly Father,[1] I want to be like David and learn to encourage myself in you.[2] Instead of being fearful, I will stand still and see your salvation and deliverance come to pass.[3] I will obey your commandment not to become discouraged in anything.[4] You have given me the strength and power I need to be strong and courageous.[5] You will never leave me nor forsake me.[6] Therefore, I will be strong in you and in the power of Your might.[7] You are the strength of my heart, and my portion forever.[8] Thank you, Lord. Amen.

References: (1) Luke 11:2; (2) 1 Samuel 30:6; (3) Exodus 14:13; (4) Deuteronomy 1:21; (5) Deuteronomy 31:6; (6) Hebrews 13:5; (7) Ephesians 6:10; (8) Psalms 73:26.

• ENDURANCE •

Key Scripture: "Indeed we count them blessed who endure. You have heard of the perseverance of Job and seen the end intended by the Lord; that the Lord is very compassionate and merciful" (James 5:11, NKJV).

Prayer: Dear Lord,[1] I know that you will endure forever.[2] You have promised that your seed shall endure forever as well.[3] Thank you, Father. How I thank you for the promises of your Word; you have said that the end times will bring tribulation, but those who will endure unto the end shall be saved.[4] I will practice endurance, Lord, as a good soldier of Jesus Christ.[5] As I endure temptation, Lord, I will experience the happiness that comes from knowing that you love me and you have prepared a crown of life for me.[6] In Jesus' name I pray,[7] Amen.

References: (1) James 4:10; (2) Psalms 9:7; (3) Psalms 89:36; (4) Mark 13:13; (5) 2 Timothy 2:3; (6) James 1:12; (7) Acts 4:12.

• ETERNITY •

Key Scripture: "The eternal God is your refuge, And underneath are the everlasting arms; He will thrust out the enemy from before you, And will say, 'Destroy!'" (Deut. 33:27, NKJV).

Prayer: O God of my praise,[1] thank you for the eternal life you have given so freely to me through Jesus Christ, my Lord.[2] You are the high and holy one who inhabits eternity. Your name is holy, and it thrills me to realize that you choose to dwell with me. Thank you for your promise to revive my spirit as I humble myself before you.[3] Through faith I will lay hold onto the eternal life to which you've called me.[4] Thank you, Father, for the glorious assurance of eternal life.[5] In Jesus' name,[6] Amen.

References: (1) Psalms 109:1; (2) Romans 6:23; (3) Isaiah 57:15; (4) 1 Timothy 6:12; (5) 1 John 5:12; (6) John 16:23.

Prayer is asking for rain. Faith is carrying the umbrella.

Now faith is the substance of things hoped for, the evidence of things not seen (Hebrews 11:1).

• FAITH •

Key Scripture: "I have been crucified with Christ and I no longer live, but Christ lives in me. The life I live in the body, I live by faith in the Son of God, who loved me and gave himself for me" (Gal. 2:20, NIV).

Prayer: O God,[1] I come before you with boldness and confidence that results from my faith in Christ, your Son.[2] Your Word imparts faith to my heart,[3] Father, and I am determined to walk by faith, and not by sight.[4] I recognize that faith is the substance of the things I hope for and the evidence of the things I cannot see.[5] I believe in you, Father, and I know that you are a Rewarder of all those who come to you in faith.[6] Thank you for your goodness to me. In Jesus' name,[7] Amen.

References: (1) Psalms 108:1; (2) Ephesians 3:12; (3) Romans 10:17; (4) 2 Corinthians 5:7; (5) Hebrews 11:1; (6) Hebrews 11:6; (7) Acts 3:6.

• FAITHFULNESS •

Key Scripture: "Because of the Lord's great love we are not consumed, for his compassions never fail. They are new every morning; great is your faithfulness" (Lam. 3:22-23, NIV).

Prayer: God in heaven,[1] your faithfulness reaches to the clouds.[2] I want to be like you, Father; I want to be your faithful servant at all times.[3] With my mouth I will make your faithfulness known to all generations.[4] Fill me with your Spirit,[5] so that I will produce the fruit of faithfulness in all my relationships and responsibilities.[6] I realize, Lord, that being faithful requires being full of faith, and I determine to walk by faith, not by sight.[7] In Jesus' faithful name I pray,[8] Amen.

References: (1) Lamentations 3:41; (2) Psalms 36:5; (3) 1 Timothy 1:12; (4) Psalms 89:1; (5) Ephesians 5:18; (6) Galatians 5:22; (7) 2 Corinthians 5:7; (8) John 16:23.

• FAVOR •

Key Scripture: "For surely, O Lord, you bless the righteous; you surround them with your favor as with a shield" (Ps. 5:12, NIV).

Prayer: Almighty God,[1] you have granted me life and favor.[2] Thank you, Father. I will keep your commandments,[3] and walk in mercy and truth.[4] In this way I know I will find favor in your sight.[5] When I found you, Lord, I found life, and I received your favor.[6] You surround me with your favor as a shield.[7] Hallelujah! Your loving favor is more important to me than all the gold and riches of the world.[8] Lord, help me to be like Jesus who increased in wisdom and stature, and in favor with you and man.[9] In His name I pray,[10] Amen.

References: (1) Job 13:3; (2) Job 10:12; (3) Proverbs 3:1; (4) Proverbs 3:3; (5) Proverbs 3:4; (6) Proverbs 8:35; (7) Psalms 5:12; (8) Proverbs 22:1; (9) Luke 2:52; (10) Luke 2:21.

Fear knocked at the door. Faith answered. No one was there.

(Inscription at Hind's Head Inn in England).

Be not afraid, only believe (Mark 5:36).

• FEAR •

Key Scripture: "Do not be afraid, little flock, for your Father has been pleased to give you the kingdom" (Luke 12:32, NIV).

Prayer: Father,[1] I thank you that you have not given me a spirit of fear. Rather, the spirit you have imparted to me is one of love, power, and a sound mind.[2] Your perfect love in my life casts out all fear.[3] Lord, you are my light and my salvation. Because this is true I will not fear anyone or anything.[4] My faith in you helps me to be strong and not fear because I know you, O Lord, will save me.[5] In Jesus' name I pray,[6] Amen.

References: (1) John 17:1; (2) 2 Timothy 1:7; (3) 1 John 4:18; (4) Psalms 27:1; (5) Isaiah 35:4; (6) John 16:26.

Forgiveness is the fragrance the flower sheds on the heel of the one that has crushed it.

Forbearing one another, and forgiving one another, if any man have a quarrel against any: even as Christ forgave you, so also do ye (Colossians 3:13).

• FORGIVENESS •

Key Scripture: "And be kind to one another, tenderhearted, forgiving one another, just as God in Christ forgave you" (Eph. 4:32, NKJV).

Prayer: Father,[1] I thank you that there is always forgiveness with you.[2] I know that when I confess my sins to you, you are always faithful and just to forgive me of my sins and to cleanse me from all unrighteousness.[3] Help me to walk in forgiveness, Lord, and to forgive others as you have forgiven me.[4] I receive your forgiveness, and I determine to forgive others.[5] I will walk in love, Father, because I know it is the bond of perfection.[6] In Jesus' name I pray,[7] Amen.

References: (1) Ephesians 3:14; (2) Psalms 130:4; (3) 1 John 1:9; (4) Luke 6:37; (5) Colossians 3:13; (6) Colossians 3:14; (7) John 15:16.

• FREEDOM •

Key Scripture: "Then Jesus said to those Jews who believed Him, 'If you abide in My word, you are My disciples indeed. 'And you shall know the truth, and the truth shall make you free'" (John 8:31-32, NKJV).

Prayer: Heavenly Father,[1] I celebrate my freedom because your Son has, indeed, set me free from sin.[2] With your help, I will stand fast in the liberty He has provided for me so that I will never again be entangled with any yoke of bondage.[3] Spiritual freedom is precious to me, Father, and I will never use my liberty as a license to sin; rather, I will maintain my freedom by being your servant.[4] Thank you for permitting me to enter into the glorious liberty of your children.[5] In Jesus' name I pray,[6] Amen.

References: (1) Luke 11:2; (2) John 8:36; (3) Galatians 5:1; (4) 1 Peter 2:16; (5) Romans 8:21; (6) Acts 9:15.

• FRIENDSHIP •

Key Scripture: "Greater love has no one than this, than to lay down one's life for his friends. 'You are My friends if you do whatever I command you'" (John 15:13-14, NKJV).

Prayer: O Lord my God,[1] thank you for wanting my friendship.[2] You are a friend who is much closer to me than any brother could be.[3] I realize, Lord, that friendship with the world prevents me from being your friend.[4] I want to be your friend always, and a true friend to others as well.[5] Through your grace I will be the kind of friend who loves at all times.[6] I would like others to recognize that, like Abraham, I am your friend.[7] In Jesus' name I pray,[8] Amen.

References: (1) 1 Chronicles 21:17; (2) John 15:14; (3) Proverbs 18:24; (4) James 4:4; (5) Proverbs 18:24; (6) Proverbs 17:17; (7) James 2:23; (8) Acts 4:10.

• FRUITFULNESS •

Key Scripture: "And we pray this in order that you may live a life worthy of the Lord and may please him in every way: bearing fruit in every good work, growing in the knowledge of God, being strengthened with all power according to his glorious might" (Col. 1:10-11, NIV).

Prayer: Father in heaven,[1] thank you for choosing me and ordaining me to bring forth fruit, and for promising that the fruit I bear will remain.[2] Your promise assures me that whatever I ask you in the name of Jesus will be given to me.[3] Thank you, Father. I seek your wisdom,[4] because I know that your wisdom is full of mercy and good fruits.[5] Fill me with your Spirit,[6] so that I will bear the fruit of your Spirit[7] everywhere I go. In Jesus' name,[8] Amen.

References: (1) John 17:5; (2) John 15:16; (3) John 15:16; (4) James 1:5; (5) James 3:17; (6) Ephesians 5:18; (7) Galatians 5:22; (8) John 15:16.

• GENTLENESS •

Key Scripture: "But the fruit of the Spirit is love, joy, peace, longsuffering, kindness, goodness, faithfulness, gentleness, self-control. Against such there is no law" (Gal. 5:22-23, NKJV).

Prayer: Father-God,[1] you have given me the shield of salvation, and your gentleness has made me great.[2] Thank you for the gentleness of your Son, Jesus.[3] Fill me with your Spirit, Lord,[4] so that I will be enabled to produce the fruit of gentleness in my life.[5] As your servant, Lord, I will be gentle to all I meet as a patient teacher should be.[6] I will speak evil of no one, and I will show forth meekness and gentleness to all.[7] In Jesus' name I pray,[8] Amen.

References: (1) Ephesians 1:3; (2) 2 Samuel 22:36; (3) 2 Corinthians 10:1; (4) Ephesians 5:18; (5) Galatians 5:23; (6) 2 Timothy 2:24; (7) Titus 3:2; (8) John 16:23.

• GIVING •

Key Scripture: "Give, and it will be given to you. A good measure, pressed down, shaken together and running over, will be poured into your lap" (Luke 6:38, NIV).

Prayer: O Lord,[1] thank you for loving the world so much that you *gave* your only begotten Son.[2] Help me to love so much that I will be generous also.[3] I have received so freely from your hands, Father, and I want to give freely as well.[4] I purpose in my heart to always give cheerfully[5] so that there may be an abundant supply of good works.[6] I give you my life, my time, my possessions, my future, my all.[7] In Jesus' name,[8] Amen.

References: (1) 2 Samuel 24:10; (2) John 3:16; (3) Luke 6:30; (4) Matthew 10:8; (5) 2 Corinthians 9:7; (6) 2 Corinthians 9:8; (7) 1 Corinthians 6:20; (8) John 14:13.

• GLADNESS •

Key Scripture: "You have put gladness in my heart, More than in the season that their grain and wine increased. I will both lie down in peace, and sleep; For You alone, O Lord, make me dwell in safety" (Ps. 4:7-8, NKJV).

Prayer: O Lord my God,[1] thank you for anointing me with the oil of gladness.[2] I will always serve you with gladness and come before your presence with singing.[3] The gladness you give to me is my hope, Father.[4] You have put everlasting joy upon my head, and you have given me gladness and joy.[5] I will rejoice in you always, Lord,[6] because I know your joy is my strength.[7] In the name of Jesus Christ, my Lord,[8] Amen.

References: (1) Psalms 7:3; (2) Psalms 45:7; (3) Psalms 100:2; (4) Proverbs 10:28; (5) Isaiah 51:11; (6) 1 Thessalonians 5:16; (7) Nehemiah 8:10; (8) Philippians 3:8.

• GODLINESS •

Key Scripture: "For bodily exercise profits a little, but godliness is profitable for all things, having promise of the life that now is and of that which is to come" (1 Tim. 4:8, NKJV).

Prayer: O God,[1] I pray that you will be with all who are in positions of authority so that your people will be able to lead quiet and peaceable lives in all godliness and honesty.[2] I will walk in the godliness you impart to me even though it is a great mystery to me.[3] I know that godliness with contentment is great gain for me, Father.[4] Therefore, I will pursue righteousness, godliness, faith, love, patience, and meekness[5] as I fight the good fight of faith.[6] In Jesus' name,[7] Amen.

References: (1) Hebrews 1:8; (2) 1 Timothy 2:2; (3) 1 Timothy 3:16; (4) 1 Timothy 6:6; (5) 1 Timothy 6:11; (6) 1 Timothy 6:12; (7) Acts 9:29.

• GRACE •

Key Scripture: "For it is by grace you have been saved, through faith — and this not from yourselves, it is the gift of God — not by works, so that no one can boast" (Eph. 2:8-9, NIV).

Prayer: Father,[1] you have saved me by your grace, through faith.[2] Your grace is sufficient for me in all things.[3] You are able to make all grace abound toward me, and you give me total sufficiency in all things so that I may abound to every good work.[4] Thank you for your grace, Father. As I approach your throne I have confidence that I shall always receive your grace and mercy to help me in my time of need.[5] In Jesus' name I pray,[6] Amen.

References: (1) Ephesians 2:8; (2) John 1:14; (3) 2 Corinthians 12:9; (4) 2 Corinthians 9:8; (5) Hebrews 4:16; (6) Luke 24:47.

God is not finished with you.

For we are His workmanship, created in Christ Jesus for good works, which God prepared beforehand that we should walk in them. (Ephesians 2:10, NKJV)

• GROWTH •

Key Scripture: "As newborn babes, desire the pure milk of the word, that you may grow thereby" (1 Peter 2:2, NKJV).

Prayer: Lord,[1] thank you for the gift of righteousness that enables me to flourish like a palm tree and to grow like a cedar in Lebanon.[2] I will speak the truth in love as I grow in Christ.[3] I will study your Word,[4] so that I will grow in grace and in the knowledge of my Lord and Savior, Jesus Christ.[5] In this way my faith and love will grow.[6] Thank you for building me, Father, to be your dwelling place through your Spirit.[7] In Jesus' name,[8] Amen.

References: (1) 1 Kings 21:26; (2) Psalms 92:12; (3) Ephesians 4:15; (4) 2 Timothy 2:15; (5) 2 Peter 3:18; (6) 2 Thessalonians 1:3; (7) Ephesians 2:20-22; (8) John 15:16.

• GUIDANCE •

Key Scripture: "For this God is our God for ever and ever; he will be our guide even to the end" (Ps. 48:14, NIV).

Prayer: Father of glory,[1] thank you for guiding me,[2] leading me,[3] and directing my paths.[4] Your Word is a light unto my path and a lamp unto my feet.[5] I will walk in the light of your Word throughout this day.[6] Thank you for guiding me with your eye.[7] Because of your guidance in my life I will never hunger or thirst; you will lead me with your mercy and you will guide me to the springs of water [8] Thank you for guiding me with the skillfulness of your hands.[9] In Jesus' name I pray,[10] Amen.

References: (1) Ephesians 1:17; (2) Psalms 73:24; (3) Psalms 23:1-2; (4) Proverbs 3:6; (5) Psalms 119:105; (6) 1 John 1:7; (7) Psalms 32:8; (8) Isaiah 49:10; (9) Psalms 78:72; (10) John 16:23.

• HEALING •

Key Scripture: "I am the Lord that healeth thee" (Exod. 15:26).

Prayer: Dear God, my Father,[1] I thank you for being the Lord who heals me.[2] You forgive all my iniquities and you heal all my diseases.[3] You have told me that healing is your children's bread.[4] Thank you for Jesus, the Great Physician, who loves to heal all who come to Him through faith.[5] Thank you for the Holy Spirit who provides gifts of healing for your people.[6] Whenever I encounter sickness in myself or others I will pray the prayer of faith because I know the effectual, fervent prayer of a righteous person avails much.[7] In Jesus' name,[8] Amen.

References: (1) Philippians 4:20; (2) Exodus 15:26; (3) Psalms 103:3; (4) Mark 7:24-30; (5) Matthew 8:16; (6) 1 Corinthians 12:9; (7) James 5:15-16; (8) Revelation 15:4.

Where you go hereafter depends on what you go after here.

For the wages of sin is death; but the gift of God is eternal life through Jesus Christ our Lord (Romans 6:23).

• HEAVEN •

Key Scripture: "Whom have I in heaven but You? And there is none upon earth that I desire besides You" (Ps. 73:25, NKJV).

Prayer: O Lord God,[1] your Word is forever settled in heaven,[2] where you sit upon your throne.[3] Thank you for the promise of eternal life that you have given to me.[4] I look forward to the heavenly city,[5] and the habitation you are preparing for me.[6] It is the certain knowledge of heaven, Father, that helps me to be an overcomer through the blood of Jesus and the word of my testimony.[7] Surely goodness and mercy will follow me all the days of my life, and I will dwell in your house forever.[8] In Jesus' name,[9] Amen.

References: (1) 2 Samuel 7:25; (2) Psalms 119:89; (3) Psalms 11:4; (4) Romans 6:23; (5) Revelation 3:12; (6) John 14:2; (7) Revelation 12:11; (8) Psalms 23:6; (9) John 15:16.

• HOLINESS •

Key Scripture: "Worship the Lord in the splendor of his holiness; tremble before him, all the earth" (Ps. 96:9, NIV).

Prayer: Who is like unto you, O Lord? You are glorious in holiness and you do great and mighty wonders.[1] I will give unto you the glory that is due to your name as I come before you, and I will worship you in the beauty of holiness.[2] I will walk in your way of holiness[3] because of the righteousness you have imparted to me through Jesus Christ.[4] I yield my life unto you, O Lord, so that I will be a servant of your righteousness through holiness.[5] In Jesus' name,[6] Amen.

References: (1) Exodus 15:11; (2) 1 Chronicles 16:29; (3) Isaiah 35:8; (4) Philippians 3:9; (5) Romans 6:19; (6) John 16:23.

• HONESTY •

Key Scripture: "Let us walk honestly, as in the day" (Rom. 13:13-14).

Prayer: My Father,[1] I always want to walk in honesty before you and before my fellow-man.[2] Your truth has made me free,[3] so I will always endeavor to do that which is honest.[4] I will think on things that are honest, just, pure, and of good report.[5] I will speak the truth in love.[6] I will study to be quiet, minding my own business and working with my own hands, as I endeavor to walk honestly toward others. By so doing, I know that I shall never lack anything.[7] In Jesus' name,[8] Amen.

References: (1) 1 John 10:29; (2) 2 Corinthians 8:21; (3) John 8:32; (4) 2 Corinthians 13:7; (5) Philippians 4:8; (6) Ephesians 4:15; (7) 1 Thessalonians 4:11-12; (8) John 16:26.

Faith goes up the stairs that love has made and looks out of the windows which hope has opened

(Charles Haddon Spurgeon)

Christ in you, the hope of glory
(Colossians 1:27).

• HOPE •

Key Scripture: "For the grace of God that brings salvation has appeared to all men....while we wait for the blessed hope — the glorious appearing of our great God and Savior, Jesus Christ" (Titus 2:11-13, NIV).

Prayer: Great God and Savior,[1] I hope in you, because I know you hear me when I pray.[2] I will hope continually, and praise you more and more.[3] Through your help I will be like Abraham who hoped against hope and continued to believe in hope.[4] You are my hope, Lord.[5] Fill me with the joy and peace that comes through believing, so that I will always abound in hope through the power of the Holy Spirit.[6] Through Christ my Lord,[7] Amen.

References: (1) Titus 2:13; (2) Psalms 38:15; (3) Psalms 71:14; (4) Romans 4:18; (5) 1 Timothy 1:1; (6) Romans 15:13; (7) Romans 7:25.

Some people would be completely naked if humility were their only clothing.

Be clothed with humility: for God resisteth the proud,
and giveth grace to the humble
(1 Peter 5:5).

• HUMILITY •

Key Scripture: "All of you, clothe yourselves with humility toward one another, because, 'God opposes the proud but gives grace to the humble.'" (1 Peter 5:5, NIV).

Prayer: God of Israel,[1] it is my fervent desire to serve you with all humility of mind.[2] I humbly beseech you, Lord, that I may find grace in your sight,[3] so that I will be able to fulfill your requirement to do justly, and to love mercy, and to walk humbly with you.[4] I thank you for your promise that assures me that if I will humble myself, you will exalt me.[5] It is my joy, Father, to walk in mercy, kindness, humility, meekness, patience, and forgiveness.[6] In the name of Jesus Christ, my Lord,[7] Amen.

References: (1) Numbers 16:9; (2) Acts 20:19; (3) 2 Samuel 16:4; (4) Micah 6:8; (5) Luke 14:11; (6) Colossians 3:12-13; (7) Colossians 3:24.

• IDOLATRY •

Key Scripture: "Therefore, my dear friends, flee from idolatry" (1 Cor. 10:14, NIV).

Prayer: O Lord God,[1] help me to always see clearly the relationship between rebellion, witchcraft, stubbornness, iniquity, and idolatry,[2] and how these violations of your will are directly tied to the rejection of your Word.[3] My life's desire is to walk in obedience to you, Father.[4] Thank you for leading me by your Spirit[5] so that I can always avoid all the works of the flesh, including idolatry.[6] You are my God, and I will have no other gods in my life.[7] I willingly mortify, with your help, all immorality in my life,[8] because I have put on the new man which is renewed in Jesus Christ.[9] In His name I pray,[10] Amen.

References: (1) 2 Samuel 7:28; (2) 1 Samuel 15:23; (3) 1 Samuel 15:23; (4) 1 Samuel 15:22; (5) Galatians 5:18; (6) Galatians 5:20; (7) Exodus 20:3; (8) Colossians 3:5; (9) Colossians 3:10; (10) Acts 2:21.

• INSPIRATION •

Key Scripture: "All Scripture is given by inspiration of God, and is profitable for doctrine, for reproof, for correction, for instruction in righteousness" (2 Tim. 3:16, NKJV).

Prayer: King of kings,[1] thank you for breathing life into me by your Holy Spirit who is the breath of life.[2] The inspiration you bring to my spirit gives me spiritual understanding, Father.[3] Thank you for inspiring me. You have given me life and breath[4] so that I would seek you and find you.[5] In you, O Lord, I live and move and have my being.[6] Continuously fill me with your Spirit,[7] Lord, so that, like your early disciples, I may daily experience the wind of your Spirit[8] inspiring me each and every day. In Jesus' name,[9] Amen.

References: (1) 1 Timothy 6:15; (2) Acts 17:25; (3) Job 32:8; (4) Acts 17:25; (5) Acts 17:27; (6) Acts 17:28; (7) Ephesians 5:18; (8) Acts 2:2; (9) Acts 2:38.

• INTEGRITY •

Key Scripture: "The Lord shall judge the people: judge me, O Lord, according to my righteousness, and according to mine integrity that is in me" (Ps. 7:8).

Prayer: Lord of lords,[1] some trust in chariots, and some in horses, but I will remember your name,[2] and I will let integrity and uprightness guide me as I wait on you.[3] Vindicate me, O Lord, as I walk in integrity and trust in you.[4] Your loving-kindness is always before me, and I will walk in your truth.[5] Feed me according to the integrity of my heart, and guide me by the skillfulness of your hands.[6] Through your righteousness, I will stand in my integrity, walk in it, and live by it, and I know this will guide my life.[7] Thank you, Father. In Jesus' name,[8] Amen.

References: (1) 1 Timothy 6:15; (2) Psalms 20:7; (3) Psalms 25:21; (4) Psalms 26:1; (5) Psalms 26:3; (6) Psalms 78:72; (7) Proverbs 11:3; (8) John 16:23.

• JESUS •

Key Scripture: "Jesus said to him, 'I am the way, the truth, and the life'" (John 14:6).

Prayer: Heavenly Father,[1] thank you for sending Jesus to be my Savior.[2] He is my life.[3] He is my wisdom, my sanctification, my righteousness, and my redemption.[4] He lives within me, and the life I now live I live by faith in your Son, Father. I love Him so much because He loves me and He gave himself for me.[5] He is my Lord.[6] He is my peace.[7] He is faithful, and He establishes me and guards me from the evil one.[8] In His name I pray,[9] Amen.

References: (1) Luke 11:2; (2) 1 John 4:14; (3) John 14:6; (4) 1 Corinthians 1:30; (5) Galatians 2:20; (6) Romans 10:9-10; (7) Ephesians 2:14; (8) 2 Thessalonians 3:3; (9) John 15:16.

Joy is the echo of God's life within us.

(Joseph Marmion)

The joy of the Lord is your strength
(Nehemiah 8:10).

• JOY •

Key Scripture: "You have made known to me the path of life; you will fill me with joy in your presence, with eternal pleasures at your right hand" (Ps. 16:11, NIV).

Prayer: O God, my God, you are my exceeding joy.[1] Your joy is my strength.[2] Thank you for your comfort and the abundance you give to me; these make my heart glad, fill me with thanksgiving, and surround me with the voice of melody.[3] You have given me everlasting joy, Father, and all sorrow and mourning have gone from my life.[4] Thank you, Father. I believe in your Son, Jesus Christ, and even though I have not seen Him, I love Him. My relationship with Him causes me to rejoice with an unspeakable joy that is full of glory.[5] In His name I pray,[6] Amen.

References: (1) Psalms 43:4; (2) Nehemiah 8:10; (3) Isaiah 51:3; (4) Isaiah 51:11; (5) 1 Peter 1:8; (6) John 15:16.

• JUSTIFICATION •

Key Scripture: "You were justified in the name of the Lord Jesus Christ and by the Spirit of our God" (1 Cor. 6:11, NIV).

Prayer: O Lord,[1] thank you for justifying me.[2] I know I am not justified by the works of the law, but by the faith of Jesus Christ in whom I believe with all my heart.[3] I am crucified with Him; nevertheless I live because Christ lives in me. I live by faith in Him because I know He loves me and He gave himself for me.[4] Thank you, Father, for sending Jesus who died for my sins and rose again for my justification.[5] You have justified me freely by your grace, through the redemption that is in Christ Jesus.[6] Thank you, Lord, for justifying me. In Jesus' name,[7] Amen.

References: (1) 2 Samuel 19:7; (2) Romans 8:33; (3) Galatians 2:16; (4) Galatians 2:20; (5) Romans 4:25; (6) Romans 3:23; (7) John 16:23.

• KINDNESS •

Key Scripture: "O praise the Lord, all ye nations: praise him, all ye people. for his merciful kindness is great toward us: and the truth of the Lord endureth for ever. Praise ye the Lord" (Ps. 117:1-2).

Prayer: O Lord,[1] your loving-kindness is better than life to me.[2] As one of your elect, I put on mercy, kindness, humility, meekness, and patience,[3] and I ever desire to walk in these qualities, Father. Therefore, I ask you to fill me with your Spirit[4] so that I will bear the fruit of kindness.[5] With all diligence, I will add virtue, knowledge, temperance, patience, godliness, brotherly kindness, and love to my faith.[6] In Jesus' name I pray,[7] Amen.

References: (1) Psalms 115:1; (2) Psalms 63:3; (3) Colossians 3:12; (4) Ephesians 5:18; (5) Galatians 5:22; (6) 2 Peter 1:7; (7) John 16:23.

• LIBERTY •

Key Scripture: "Because the creature itself also shall be delivered from the bondage of corruption into the glorious liberty of the children of God" (Rom. 8:21).

Prayer: Heavenly Father,[1] I will walk in your Spirit[2] because I know that where your Spirit is, there is liberty.[3] I will stand fast in the liberty you have given to me, and I will not be entangled again with the yokes of bondage which once held me back.[4] Thank you for calling me to true spiritual freedom, Lord. I cherish this liberty, and I never want to use it as an opportunity to sin.[5] I will continue to look into your perfect law of liberty (your Word). I will not forget your promises to me. I will do the work you've given me to do, and I know I shall be blessed.[6] Thank you, Master. In Jesus' name,[7] Amen.

References: (1) Philippians 1:2; (2) Galatians 5:16; (3) 2 Corinthians 3:17; (4) Galatians 5:1; (5) Galatians 5:13; (6) James 1:25; (7) John 15:16.

• LOVE •

Key Scripture: "And so we know and rely on the love God has for us. God is love. Whoever lives in love lives in God, and God in him" (1 John 4:16, NIV).

Prayer: Loving Father,[1] I thank you for the certain knowledge that nothing shall be able to separate me from your love which I have found in Christ Jesus, my Lord.[2] In fact, I am more than a conqueror through your Son, Jesus, who loved me enough to die for me.[3] My heart's desire, Father, is to love you with all my heart, soul, and mind, and to love other people as I love myself.[4] Teach me your more-excellent way.[5] As I pray, I sense your love being poured forth in my heart by the Holy Spirit who dwells within me.[6] I love you, Lord, because I know you first loved me.[7] In Jesus' name,[8] Amen.

References: (1) John 6:65; (2) Romans 8:39; (3) Romans 8:37; (4) Matthew 22:37-39; (5) 1 Corinthians 12:31; (6) Romans 5:5; (7) 1 John 4:19; (8) John 16:26.

• LOVINGKINDNESS •

Key Scripture: "Because Your lovingkindness is better than life, My lips shall praise You" (Ps. 63:3, NKJV).

Prayer: O Lord,[1] your lovingkindness is before my eyes, and I have walked in your truth.[2] How excellent is your lovingkindness, O God. Because of it I am able to put my complete trust in you as I rest secure under your wings.[3] Let your lovingkindness and your truth continually preserve me, Father.[4] I will show forth your lovingkindness in the morning and your faithfulness every night.[5] Thank you, Lord, for redeeming my life from destruction and crowning me with your lovingkindness and tender mercies.[6] Truly, your lovingkindness is better than life to me.[7] In Jesus' name,[8] Amen.

References: (1) Psalms 120:2; (2) Psalms 26:3; (3) Psalms 36:7; (4) Psalms 40:11; (5) Psalms 92:2; (6) Psalms 103:4; (7) Psalms 63:3; (8) Philippians 2:9.

• MAJESTY •

Key Scripture: "Yours, O Lord, is the greatness, the power and the glory, the victory and the majesty" (1 Chron. 29:11, NKJV).

Prayer: O Lord God, my Father,[1] your voice is full of majesty and power.[2] You reign over all, and you are clothed with strength and majesty.[3] I will extoll you, my God and King. Your greatness is truly unsearchable. I will speak of the glorious honor of your majesty and of all your mighty works.[4] I know you are able to keep me from falling and to present me faultless before the presence of your glory with exceeding joy. To you, the only wise God, my Savior, be glory and majesty, dominion, and power both now and forevermore.[5] In Jesus' name,[6] Amen.

References: (1) 1 Chronicles 29:11; (2) Psalms 29:4; (3) Psalms 93:1; (4) Psalms 145:1-5; (5) Jude 24-25; (6) John 15:16.

• MEDITATION •

Key Scripture: "Let the words of my mouth and the meditation of my heart Be acceptable in Your sight, O Lord, my strength and my Redeemer" (Ps. 19:14, NKJV).

Prayer: Heavenly Father,[1] my delight is in your Word, and in your Word I will meditate both day and night.[2] Through Word-centered meditation, I know I shall become like a tree planted by the rivers of water. I will bear good fruit and my leaf will not wither. In fact, I will prosper in whatever I do.[3] Thank you for this promise of your Word, Father. I will continually meditate upon the precepts of your Word,[4] and I will give myself wholly to them.[5] My meditation of you and your Word will always be sweet, and I will always be glad in you.[6] In Jesus' name I pray,[7] Amen.

References: (1) Matthew 16:17; (2) Psalms 1:2; (3) Psalms 1:3; (4) Psalms 119:15; (5) 1 Timothy 4:15; (6) Psalms 104:34; (7) Luke 2:21.

• MEEKNESS •

Key Scripture: "Seek ye the Lord, all ye meek of the earth, which have wrought his judgment; seek righteousness, seek meekness" (Zeph. 2:3).

Prayer: O Lord,[1] help me to walk in meekness at all times. I know you will guide the meek in judgment,[2] that I will eat and be satisfied,[3] and you will teach me your way if I walk in meekness.[4] You have even promised that the meek will inherit the earth.[5] You will lift up the meek,[6] and you will beautify the meek with your salvation.[7] As I walk in meekness, Father, I am filled with joy.[8] I will put on the meekness you provide to me through your Holy Spirit.[9] In Jesus' name,[10] Amen.

References: (1) Psalms 135:13; (2) Psalms 25:9; (3) Psalms 22:26; (4) Psalms 25:9; (5) Psalms 37:11; (6) Psalms 147:6; (7) Psalms 149:4; (8) Isaiah 29:19; (9) Colossians 3:12; (10) Matthew 1:23.

• MERCY •

Key Scripture: "In his great mercy he has given us new birth into a living hope through the resurrection of Jesus Christ from the dead" (1 Peter 1:3-4, NIV).

Prayer: Heavenly Father,[1] thank you for having mercy upon me.[2] I trust in your mercy, Lord, and my heart rejoices in your salvation.[3] Your abundant mercy keeps me from slipping and falling.[4] I know that you will perfect those things that pertain to me because I know that your mercy endures forever.[5] Your goodness and mercy will follow me all the days of my life, and I will dwell in your house forever.[6] Father, you are rich in mercy which you have revealed through your great love.[7] Thank you for your mercy and love. In Jesus' name,[8] Amen.

References: (1) 1 Thessalonians 1:1; (2) Psalms 6:12; (3) Psalms 13:5; (4) Psalms 94:18; (5) Psalms 138:8; (6) Psalms 23:6; (7) Ephesians 2:4; (8) John 16:23.

• MONEY •

Key Scripture: "For the love of money is a root of all kinds of evil, for which some have strayed from the faith in their greediness, and pierced themselves through with many sorrows" (1 Tim. 6:10, NKJV).

Prayer: Father God,[1] as I seek you and your righteousness first,[2] I know that all I need, including financial resources, will be supplied to me.[3] I know you know what I need even before I express it to you.[4] The money I have does not belong to me, Lord; so I ask you to help me to be a good steward of all you give to me.[5] Help me to give cheerfully,[6] to lay up treasures in heaven rather than on earth,[7] and to use and invest my resources wisely.[8] In Jesus' name,[9] Amen.

References: (1) John 3:35; (2) Matthew 6:33; (3) Philippians 4:19; (4) Matthew 6:8; (5) Psalms 50:10; (6) 2 Corinthians 9:7; (7) Matthew 6:20; (8) Matthew 25; (9) Acts 2:21.

• NEIGHBORS •

Key Scripture: "Do not forsake your friend and the friend of your father, and do not go to your brother's house when disaster strikes you — better a neighbor nearby than a brother far away" (Prov. 27:10, NIV).

Prayer: Thank you for my neighbors, Father.[1] Bless my neighbors, _____ _____, with all spiritual blessings in heavenly places in Christ.[2] Help me to love my neighbor as myself,[3] to fulfill your law by always being good to my neighbor,[4] to please my neighbor by encouraging him/her,[5] to be certain to speak truth to my neighbor,[6] and to teach my neighbor about your gospel and your truth.[7] In Jesus' name I pray,[8] Amen.

References: (1) Philippians 1:2; (2) Ephesians 1:3; (3) Mark 12:31; (4) Romans 13:10; (5) Romans 15:2; (6) Ephesians 4:25; (7) Hebrews 8:11; (8) John 15:16.

• OBEDIENCE •

Key Scripture: "For as by one man's disobedience many were made sinners, so also by one Man's obedience many will be made righteous" (Rom. 5:19, NKJV).

Prayer: O Lord,[1] thank you for Jesus Christ who learned obedience through the things that He suffered.[2] It is my desire, Father, to be like Him, to walk in obedience to your perfect will.[3] Thank you for freeing me from sin, Lord, and making me a servant of your righteousness.[4] Throughout my life I will delight in doing your will.[5] I pray that I will always be able to say, "I have obeyed the voice of the Lord, and have gone the way which the Lord sent me." Through Christ, my Lord,[6] Amen.

References: (1) Luke 5:8; (2) Hebrews 5:8; (3) Psalms 18:44; (4) Romans 6:17-18; (5) Psalms 40:8; (6) Galatians 6:14.

• PATIENCE •

Key Scripture: "For ye have need of patience, that, after ye have done the will of God, ye might receive the promise" (Heb. 10:36).

Prayer: Living God,[1] through faith and patience I will receive your promises.[2] Thank you for the promises of your Word which are yes and amen in Christ Jesus.[3] I will run with patience the race you have set before me, looking unto Jesus who is the Author and Finisher of my faith.[4] Realizing that the trying of my faith works patience into my life, I will let patience have its perfect work within me so that I will be complete in Christ, lacking nothing.[5] Through keeping your word of patience, Father, you will keep me from the hour of temptation.[6] In Jesus' name,[7] Amen.

References: (1) Hebrews 11:6; (2) Hebrews 6:12; (3) 2 Corinthians 1:20; (4) Hebrews 12:1-2; (5) James 1:2-3; (6) Revelation 3:10; (7) John 15:16.

• PEACE •

Key Scripture: "The Lord gives strength to his people; the Lord blesses his people with peace" (Ps. 29:11, NIV).

Prayer: O Lord,[1] thank you for calling me to peace,[2] and for filling me with your Spirit[3] so that I would be able to bear the fruit of peace in my life.[4] Through Christ, you have given me your peace, and this keeps my heart from being troubled.[5] Truly, your peace, Lord, goes beyond my understanding.[6] As I continue to walk in your Spirit,[7] and cultivate spiritual-mindedness in my life, I know that I will have life and peace.[8] Through Christ, my Lord,[9] Amen.

References: (1) Psalms 31:1; (2) 1 Corinthians 7:15; (3) Ephesians 5:18; (4) Galatians 5:22; (5) John 14:27; (6) Philippians 4:7; (7) Galatians 5:16; (8) Romans 8:6; (9) Ephesians 3:14.

We are to take care of the possible and let God take care of the impossible.

(Ruth Bell Graham)

All things are possible to him that believeth
(Mark 9:23).

• POSSIBILITY •

Key Scripture: "With man this is impossible, but not with God; all things are possible with God" (Mark 10:27, NIV).

Prayer: Heavenly Father,[1] with you all things are truly possible.[2] You have assured me, Lord, that all things are possible to me as well — when I truly believe.[3] Your kingdom is the land of infinite possibilities, and as I cry Abba, Father, I realize anew that there are no impossibilities in you.[4] Those things that seem impossible to human beings are possible with you.[5] Your Word declares that I can do all things through Christ who strengthens me,[6] for greater is He that is in me than He that is in the world.[7] In Jesus' name,[8] Amen.

References: (1) Luke 11:2; (2) Matthew 19:26; (3) Mark 9:23; (4) Mark 14:36; (5) Luke 18:27; (6) Philippians 4:13; (7) 1 John 4:4; (8) John 16:23.

• POWER •

Key Scripture: "Great is our Lord and mighty in power; his understanding has no limit" (Ps. 147:5, NIV).

Prayer: O Father,[1] you rule by your power forever,[2] and you give strength and power to me.[3] I thank you that your Gospel reveals your power unto salvation to all who believe.[4] As I study your powerful Word,[5] let your Spirit enlighten the eyes of my understanding so that I will fully know the hope of my calling, the riches of the glory of your inheritance in my life,[6] and the exceeding greatness of your power toward me, Lord.[7] In Jesus' name I pray,[8] Amen.

References: (1) Luke 10:21; (2) Psalms 66:7; (3) Psalms 68:35; (4) Romans 1:16; (5) Hebrews 4:12; (6) Ephesians 1:18; (7) Ephesians 1:19; (8) John 15:16.

• PRAISE •

Key Scripture: "Sing praises to God, sing praises; sing praises to our King, sing praises. For God is the King of all the earth; sing to him a psalm of praise" (Ps. 47:6-7, NIV).

Prayer: Lord God, the Mighty One,[1] how good it is to sing praises to you; it is fitting and it is pleasant for me to praise you.[2] Every day I will praise you, and I will extol your name forever and ever.[3] You are so great and you are greatly to be praised.[4] No one can truly fathom your greatness, Father.[5] You send your commands to the earth, and your Word runs swiftly.[6] I will praise you all my life, and I will sing praises to you as long as I live.[7] Thank you, Lord. In Jesus' name,[8] Amen.

References: (1) Psalms 50:1; (2) Psalms 147:1; (3) Psalms 145:1-2; (4) Psalms 48:1; (5) Psalms 145:3; (6) Psalms 147:15; (7) Psalms 146:2; (8) John 16:23.

More things are wrought by prayer than this world dreams of.

(Alfred, Lord Tennyson)

Call unto me, and I will answer thee, and shew thee great and mighty things, which thou knowest not (Jeremiah 33:3).

• PRAYER •

Key Scripture: "Pray continually; give thanks in all circumstances, for this is God's will for you in Christ Jesus" (1 Thess. 5:16-18, NIV).

Prayer: Heavenly Father,[1] I thank you for the prayer promises of your Word.[2] When I come before you in prayer I do so in faith, knowing that you are there and that you are a Rewarder of all those who diligently seek you.[3] Through prayer, Lord, I seek you and your will, and as I do so, I know that you are fully aware of all my needs even before I express them to you.[4] Through prayer I get to know you as my "Abba, Father,"[5] the One who supplies all my needs according to your riches in Christ Jesus.[6] In His name I pray,[7] Amen.

References: (1) Luke 11:2; (2) 2 Peter 1:4; (3) Hebrews 11:6; (4) Matthew 6:8; (5) Galatians 4:6; (6) Philippians 4:19; (7) John 16:26.

His [God's] promise is a threefold cord that cannot be broken.

(Andrew Murray)

And all things, whatsoever ye shall ask in prayer, believing, ye shall receive (Matthew 21:22).

• PROMISES •

Key Scripture: "For all the promises of God in Him are Yes, and in Him Amen, to the glory of God through us" (2 Cor. 1:20, NKJV).

Prayer: O Lord, you are my God,[1] Your counsels of old are faithfulness and truth.[2] Because I believe all the promises of your Word, I want to be whole, Lord; I want to experience the perfection, holiness, and completion that your Word promises to me.[3] I thank you that there is no law against your promises.[4] By the exercise of my faith and patience I will inherit all your promises.[5] Thank you for giving me so many exceedingly great and precious promises.[6] In Jesus' name I pray,[7] Amen.

References: (1) Isaiah 25:1; (2) Isaiah 25:1; (3) 2 Corinthians 7:1; (4) Galatians 3:21; (5) Hebrews 6:12; (6) 2 Peter 1:3-4; (7) John 15:16.

Prayer is the golden key that opens heaven.

(Thomas Watson)

And he shall be like a tree planted by the rivers of water, that bringeth forth his fruit in his season; his leaf also shall not wither; and whatsoever he doeth shall prosper (Psalms 1:3).

• PROSPERITY •

Key Scripture: "Therefore keep the words of this covenant, and do them, that you may prosper in all that you do" (Deut. 29:9, NKJV).

Prayer: O God,[1] thank you for the promises of prosperity that your Word declares to me. You make my way prosperous.[2] I take delight in your Word by meditating upon your promises both day and night.[3] Thank you for making me like a tree that is planted by the rivers of water — a fruitful tree that produces abundant prosperity.[4] I will always seek you first, Lord, and your righteousness, and I know that the result of my seeking will be full and overflowing provision.[5] Great is your faithfulness;[6] you will always supply all my needs according to your riches in glory through Jesus Christ, my Lord.[7] Amen.

References: (1) Psalms 74:10; (2) Joshua 1:8; (3) Psalms 1:2; (4) Psalms 1:3; (5) Matthew 6:33; (6) Lamentations 3:23; (7) Philippians 4:19.

• PROTECTION •

Key Scripture: "The beloved of the Lord shall dwell in safety by him; and the Lord shall cover him all the day long" (Deut. 33:12).

Prayer: O God of my salvation,[1] thank you for your constant protection in my life.[2] I dwell in your safety.[3] I will listen for your voice at all times, and this will keep me in your safe-keeping where I can live securely.[4] I will walk in my way safely because I know you are with me.[5] When I lie down I will not be afraid and my sleep will be sweet.[6] You are my complete confidence, Lord, and because of your safe-keeping I have absolutely no fear of sudden disaster or of the ruin that overtakes the wicked.[7] Thank you for your protection in my life. In Jesus' name,[8] Amen.

References: (1) 1 Chronicles 16:35; (2) Deuteronomy 32:28; (3) Deuteronomy 33:12; (4) Proverbs 1:33; (5) Proverbs 3:23; (6) Proverbs 3:24; (7) Proverbs 3:25-26; (8) Acts 4:12.

• PURITY •

Key Scripture: "To the pure, all things are pure, but to those who are corrupted and do not believe, nothing is pure" (Titus 1:15, NIV).

Prayer: Maker of heaven and earth,[1] help me to love you and to love others with a pure heart.[2] I know, Father, that purity comes from obeying the truth through your Spirit.[3] Thank you for the purity of your wisdom, Lord.[4] I choose to think about pure things — those things that are honest, just, lovely, and of good report.[5] In so doing, I know I will be able to call upon you with a pure heart,[6] a pure conscience,[7] and a pure mind.[8] In Jesus' name,[9] Amen.

References: (1) Psalms 121:2; (2) 1 Peter 1:22; (3) 1 Peter 1:22; (4) James 3:17; (5) Philippians 4:8; (6) 1 Peter 1:22; (7) 2 Timothy 1:3; (8) 2 Peter 3:1; (9) John 15:16.

• QUIETNESS •

Key Scripture: "In repentance and rest is your salvation, in quietness and trust is your strength" (Isa. 30:15, NIV).

Prayer: Lord Almighty,[1] you are my Shepherd and because this is true, I will never want for anything.[2] You make me lie down in green pastures, and you lead me beside the still and quiet waters.[3] You restore my soul.[4] I hearken to you, Lord, and as I do so, I find that place of quiet rest near to your heart because you keep me safe and secure, and you keep my heart quiet from all fear of evil.[5] I will study to be quiet, and to mind my own business, because I know these behaviors will lead to greater peace in my life.[6] Thank you, Father. In Jesus' name I pray,[7] Amen.

References: (1) Isaiah 28:22; (2) Psalms 23:1; (3) Psalms 23:2; (4) Psalms 23:3; (5) Proverbs 1:33; (6) 1 Thessalonians 4:11; (7) John 15:16.

• REBELLION •

Key Scripture: "For rebellion is as the sin of witchcraft, And stubbornness is as iniquity and idolatry. Because you have rejected the word of the Lord, He also has rejected you from being king" (1 Sam. 15:23, NKJV).

Prayer: Hear, O Lord, and answer me.[1] I never want to disobey you or your Word.[2] To do so, I realize, is to rebel against you.[3] I will walk in obedience to you and your Word.[4] I will cast down all vain imaginations and every other thing that exalts itself against knowing you, Father, and I will bring all my thoughts into obedience to Christ.[5] When I fall, I will confess my sins to you, knowing that you will forgive me of my sins and cleanse me from all unrighteousness.[6] Through Jesus Christ, my Lord,[7] Amen.

References: (1) Psalms 86:1; (2) Psalms 107:11; (3) Psalms 5:10; (4) 2 John 6; (5) 2 Corinthians 10:5; (6) 1 John 1:9; (7) Galatians 1:3.

• REDEMPTION •

Key Scripture: "For I know that my Redeemer lives, And He shall stand at last on the earth" (Job 19:25, NKJV).

Prayer: Let the words of my mouth, and the meditation of my heart, be acceptable in your sight, O Lord, my strength, and my Redeemer.[1] You are my mighty Redeemer,[2] and I will always proclaim this because you have delivered me from the hands of the enemy.[3] Christ has redeemed me from the curse of the Law by becoming cursed on the tree of Calvary in my behalf.[4] He bought me with the price of His blood,[5] and as a result, the blessing of Abraham comes upon me as I receive your promises by faith.[6] In Jesus' name,[7] Amen.

References: (1) Psalms 19:14; (2) Proverbs 23:11; (3) Psalms 107:2; (4) Galatians 3:13; (5) 1 Corinthians 6:20; (6) Galatians 3:14; (7) John 15:16.

• REDEEMER •

Key Scripture: "Their Redeemer is strong; The Lord of hosts is His name. He will thoroughly plead their case, That He may give rest to the land, And disquiet the inhabitants of Babylon" (Jer. 50:34, NKJV).

Prayer: Lord of hosts,[1] you are my Redeemer.[2] I know that my body is the temple of the Holy Spirit who dwells within me.[3] This is possible because Jesus Christ bought me back from the enemy with His blood.[4] Therefore, I will glorify Him in my body and my spirit because I now realize that all I am and have is yours.[5] I know that my Redeemer lives.[6] He has defeated the last enemy — death — and He has given me complete spiritual victory in every area of my life.[7] Thank you, Father. I love you. In Jesus' name I pray,[8] Amen.

References: (1) Jeremiah 50:33; (2) Job 19:25; (3) 1 Corinthians 6:19; (4) 1 Peter 1:19; (5) 1 Corinthians 6:20; (6) Revelation 1:18; (7) 1 Corinthians 15:54-58; (8) John 16:23.

I am oftimes driven to my knees by the overwhelming conviction that I have nowhere else to go.

(Abraham Lincoln)

The prayer of a righteous man is powerful and effective
(James 5:16, NIV).

• REFUGE •

Key Scripture: "God is our refuge and strength, an ever-present help in trouble. Therefore we will not fear, though the earth give way and the mountains fall into the heart of the sea" (Ps. 46:1-2, NIV).

Prayer: O Lord my God,[1] you are a refuge for the oppressed,[2] the poor,[3] and you are my refuge and my portion in the land of the living.[4] You are my safe place, and on you alone will I wait, for I expect great things from you.[5] You are my rock, Father, and you are my salvation. In fact, you are my total defense; therefore, I shall not be moved. I find all my strength in you, Lord, and I will trust in you at all times. I will pour out my heart to you through prayer, for you are my eternal refuge.[6] In Jesus' name,[7] Amen.

References: (1) 1 Kings 17:20; (2) Psalms 9:9; (3) Psalms 14:6; (4) Psalms 142:5; (5) Psalms 62:5; (6) Psalms 62:6-8; (7) John 15:16.

• REJOICING •

Key Scripture: "Rejoice in the Lord and be glad, you righteous; sing, all you who are upright in heart!" (Ps. 32:11, NIV).

Prayer: Dear God, you are the Mighty One; God, you are the Lord.[1] I will be glad and rejoice in you.[2] I rejoice in your salvation and in your name.[3] My soul waits for you, O Lord, for you are my help and my shield.[4] My heart shall always rejoice in you because I trust you in everything.[5] I will bless you at all times, Lord, and your praise shall continually be in my mouth.[6] My soul will make its boast in you as I magnify your name.[7] I will rejoice in you always, Father, and I will keep on doing so as long as I live.[8] Through Christ, my Lord,[9] Amen.

References: (1) Psalms 50:1; (2) Psalms 9:2; (3) Psalms 20:5; (4) Psalms 33:20; (5) Psalms 33:21; (6) Psalms 34:1; (7) Psalms 34:2-3; (8) Philippians 4:4; (9) Philippians 3:3.

• RENEWAL •

Key Scripture: "Create in me a clean heart, O God, And renew a steadfast spirit within me" (Ps. 51:10, NKJV).

Prayer: God of my salvation,[1] as I wait upon you I know you will renew my strength. You will enable me to mount up with wings like an eagle, and I will be able to run and not be weary, to walk and not faint.[2] I thank you that my youth is renewed as the eagle's,[3] and my inner man is renewed day by day.[4] Continue to renew me in the spirit of my mind[5] through the washing of the water of your Word.[6] Heavenly Father, I choose to put on the new man which is renewed in knowledge after your image.[7] Thank you for continually renewing me, Lord. In Jesus' name I pray,[8] Amen.

References: (1) Psalms 51:14; (2) Isaiah 40:31; (3) Psalms 103:5; (4) 2 Corinthians 4:16; (5) Ephesians 4:23; (6) Ephesians 5:26; (7) Colossians 3:10; (8) John 15:7.

To do it no more is the truest repentance.

(Martin Luther)

*Godly sorrow worketh repentance
(2 Corinthians 7:10).*

• REPENTANCE •

Key Scripture: "Therefore bear fruits worthy of repentance" (Matt. 3:8, NKJV).

Prayer: Our Father who lives in heaven,[1] thank you for giving me the ability to repent of my sins.[2] I now repent of all my unconfessed sins. Your goodness in my life leads me to repentance.[3] Thank you for the godly sorrow that leads me to repent when I sin. It leads me to life and peace.[4] Through the gift of repentance, you enable me to acknowledge the truth,[5] and this truth will make me free.[6] I thank you, Father, that you are never slack concerning your promises, but you are patient toward me, and you draw me to repentance.[7] Through Jesus Christ, my Lord,[8] Amen.

References: (1) Matthew 6:1; (2) Acts 5:31; (3) Romans 2:4; (4) 2 Corinthians 7:10; (5) 2 Timothy 2:25; (6) John 8:32; (7) 2 Peter 3:9; (8) Acts 2:36.

• REST •

Key Scripture: "Come to me, all you who are weary and burdened, and I will give you rest. Take my yoke upon you and learn from me, for I am gentle and humble in heart, and you will find rest for your souls" (Matt. 11:28-29, NIV).

Prayer: O sovereign Lord,[1] thank you for the example you've given to me concerning the importance of rest in my life. After your works of creation were finished, you rested on the seventh day, and you said that it was holy.[2] By trusting you and keeping my mind stayed upon you I can experience rest every day.[3] Thank you for your promise that I am able to enter into your rest.[4] I choose to enter the rest you have provided for me, Father, by ceasing from my own works,[5] keeping my heart open to you,[6] and obeying you.[7] In Jesus' name,[8] Amen.

References: (1) Psalms 141:8; (2) Genesis 2:2; (3) Isaiah 26:3; (4) Hebrews 4:1; (5) Hebrews 4:10; (6) Hebrews 4:7; (7) Hebrews 4:11; (8) John 15:16.

• RESTORATION •

Key Scripture: "Your people will rebuild the ancient ruins and will raise up the age-old foundations; you will be called Repairer of Broken Walls, Restorer of Streets with Dwellings" (Isa. 58:12, NIV).

Prayer: Blessed Redeemer,[1] your wonderful Word abounds with promises of restoration. You restore my soul.[2] You restore my life, and you will nourish me in my old age.[3] You restore health to me.[4] Thank you for your promise that you will restore years to me after calamity,[5] you restore the joy of thy salvation,[6] and you will renew my youth.[7] I look forward to the day, Father, when you will restore your kingdom here on earth.[8] In Jesus' name,[9] Amen.

References: (1) Isaiah 59:20; (2) Psalms 23:3; (3) Ruth 4:15; (4) Jeremiah 30:17; (5) Joel 2:25; (6) Psalms 51:12; (7) Psalms 103:5; (8) Daniel 9:25; (9) John 14:13.

• RESURRECTION •

Key Scripture: "And whoever lives and believes in Me shall never die. Do you believe this?" (John 11:26, NKJV).

Prayer: Lord God of hosts,[1] thank you for the glorious message and meaning of Easter: Jesus Christ is risen indeed![2] Because He lives,[3] I can face tomorrow. Because He lives, all fear is gone.[4] Death no longer has any sting for me because He lives.[5] The grave is no longer victorious.[6] I thank you, Father, for giving me complete victory through Jesus Christ, my Lord.[7] Thank you for reserving a place in heaven for me.[8] In Jesus; name,[9] Amen.

References: (1) Jeremiah 50:25; (2) Matthew 28:6; (3) John 11:25; (4) 1 John 4:18; (5) 1 Corinthians 15:55; (6) 1 Corinthians 15:55; (7) 1 Corinthians 15:57; (8) 1 Peter 1:4; (9) John 14:14.

• REVELATION •

Key Scripture: "I keep asking that the God of our Lord Jesus Christ, the glorious Father, may give you the Spirit of wisdom and revelation, so that you may know him better" (Eph. 1:17, NIV).

Prayer: Glorious Father,[1] I thank you for giving me the spirit of wisdom and revelation in the knowledge of You,[2] the eyes of my understanding being enlightened so that I will know the hope of Your calling and what are the riches of the glory of Your inheritance.[3] You are revealing to me the exceeding greatness of your power toward me as I exercise my faith in Jesus Christ.[4] Through your grace I am receiving spiritual revelation day by day, and you are revealing your mysteries to me.[5] Thank you, Father. In Jesus' name,[6] Amen.

References: (1) Ephesians 1:17; (2) Ephesians 1:17; (3) Ephesians 1:18; (4) Ephesians 1:19; (5) Ephesians 3:3; (6) John 14:13.

• REVIVAL •

Key Scripture: "Will You not revive us again, That Your people may rejoice in You? Show us Your mercy, Lord, And grant us Your salvation" (Ps. 85:6-7, NKJV).

Prayer: God of hope,[1] thank you for your promise of revival.[2] Revive our land,[3] Lord, and let that revival begin in me.[4] Though I walk in the midst of trouble, I know you will revive me. You will stretch forth your hand against the wrath of my enemies, and your right hand will save me.[5] I will walk in humility before you, Father, because I know your promise is to revive my spirit and my heart if I will do so.[6] Thank you for your mercy that brings revival to me. Set up your kingdom in our land. Repair the spiritual desolation of a land that has been laid waste by the enemy.[7] In Jesus' name I pray,[8] Amen.

References: (1) Romans 15:13; (2) Hosea 14:7; (3) Hosea 6:2; (4) Isaiah 57:15; (5) Psalms 138:7; (6) Isaiah 57:15; (7) Ezra 9:9; (8) John 16:23.

• RIGHTEOUSNESS •

Key Scripture: "But seek first his kingdom and his righteousness, and all these things will be given to you as well" (Matt. 6:33-34, NIV).

Prayer: O God of my righteousness,[1] lead me in your righteousness[2] and the ways of your kingdom.[3] You are my righteousness, and through your gracious love you have made me the righteousness of God in Christ.[4] Lord, I want to always be found in Christ, not having my own righteousness which is of the law but having the righteousness which is through faith in Jesus Christ, the righteousness which is from you by faith.[5] I confess my sins to you, God, and in your faithfulness and justice you cleanse me from all unrighteousness.[6] In Jesus' name,[7] Amen.

References: (1) Psalms 4:1; (2) Psalms 5:8; (3) Matthew 6:30; (4) 2 Corinthians 5:21; (5) Philippians 3:9; (6) 1 John 1:9; (7) John 15:7.

Born once, die twice; born twice, die once.

Except a man be born again, he cannot see the kingdom of God (John 3:3).

• SALVATION •

Key Scripture: "For I am not ashamed of the gospel of Christ, for it is the power of God to salvation for everyone who believes, for the Jew first and also for the Greek" (Rom. 1:16, NKJV).

Prayer: O Lord,[1] how I praise you for your so-great salvation.[2] With my heart I have believed unto righteousness, and with my mouth I have made a public confession of my salvation.[3] I confess the Lord Jesus Christ as my Savior, and I believe in my heart that you have raised Him from the dead.[4] Therefore, I know I have eternal life.[5] Your saving power keeps me as I exercise faith in your promises.[6] In Jesus' name I pray,[7] Amen.

References: (1) Joshua 7:8; (2) Hebrews 2:3; (3) Romans 10:10; (4) Romans 10:9; (5) 1 John 2:25; (6) John 15:7; (7) John 15:16.

• SANCTIFICATION •

Key Scripture: "But of Him you are in Christ Jesus, who became for us wisdom from God; and righteousness and sanctification and redemption" (1 Cor. 1:30, NKJV).

Prayer: Father-God,[1] I thank you that Jesus is my righteousness, sanctification, and redemption.[2] I praise you, Lord, because you chose me from the beginning to receive your salvation through sanctification of the Spirit and believing the truth.[3] I believe the truth of your Word, Father, and it has made me free.[4] Thank you for washing me in the water of your Word,[5] and sanctifying and justifying me through the power of the Holy Spirit.[6] In Jesus' name,[7] Amen.

References: (1) 1 Corinthians 1:3; (2) 1 Corinthians 1:30; (3) 2 Thessalonians 2:13; (4) John 8:32; (5) Ephesians 5:26; (6) Romans 15:16; (7) John 16:23.

• SELF-CONTROL •

Key Scripture: "But the fruit of the Spirit is love, joy, peace, longsuffering, gentleness, goodness, faith, meekness, temperance: against such there is no law" (Gal. 5:22).

Prayer: Sovereign Lord,[1] thank you for your exceedingly great and precious promises.[2] With all diligence I will add virtue to my faith and knowledge to my virtue.[3] To my knowledge I will add self-control, and to my self-control I will add patience. Then to my patience I will add godliness.[4] To the godliness you impart to me I will add brotherly kindness, and to brotherly kindness I will add love.[5] Self-control will help me to achieve these goals through Christ, my Lord.[6] Amen.

References: (1) Ezekiel 44:27; (2) 2 Peter 1:4; (3) 2 Peter 1:5; (4) 2 Peter 1:6; (5) 2 Peter 1:7; (6) 1 Peter 5:14.

• SERVING •

Key Scripture: "Be devoted to one another in brotherly love. Honor one another above yourselves. Never be lacking in zeal, but keep your spiritual fervor, serving the Lord" (Rom. 12:10-11, NIV).

Prayer: Father of glory,[1] give me a servant's heart as I endeavor to serve you and others. I will serve you by following Jesus Christ in all that I say and do.[2] I belong to you, Father, and I will serve you throughout my life.[3] Thank you for calling me to liberty; I will not use my liberty as an occasion to sin, but to serve others through the love you impart to me.[4] It is thrilling for me to realize that I will receive the reward of your spiritual inheritance as I continue to serve the Lord Christ.[5] Thank you, Father. In Jesus' name,[6] Amen.

References: (1) Ephesians 1:17; (2) John 12:26; (3) Acts 27:23; (4) Galatians 5:13; (5) Colossians 3:24; (6) John 16:23.

• SICKNESS •

Key Scripture: "Worship the Lord your God, and his blessing will be on your food and water. I will take away sickness from among you, and none will miscarry or be barren in your land. I will give you a full life span" (Exod. 23:25-26, NIV).

Prayer: Jehovah-Rapha, you are my Healer.[1] Thank you for all the promises your Word contains about health and healing. I know you will take away all sicknesses from me, and you will put no diseases upon me.[2] Thank you, Father. Your Son, my Lord and Savior, Jesus Christ, took all my sicknesses upon himself when He died for me.[3] By His stripes I am healed.[4] He is able to heal all manner of sickness and disease.[5] I receive His healing power as I pray. In Jesus' name,[6] Amen.

References: (1) Jeremiah 30:17; (2) Deuteronomy 7:15; (3) Matthew 8:17; (4) Isaiah 53:5; (5) Matthew 10:1; (6) John 15:7.

• SIMPLICITY •

Key Scripture: "But I fear, lest somehow, as the serpent deceived Eve by his craftiness, so your minds may be corrupted from the simplicity that is in Christ" (2 Cor. 11:3, NKJV).

Prayer: O my God,[1] your Word is perfect and it gives me wisdom.[2] When I walk in simplicity, your Word declares, you will preserve me. When I am brought low, you will lift me up.[3] I thank you that you give understanding to me as I walk in simplicity before you. Your Word gives light to my spirit.[4] I rejoice in you, Father. The testimony of my conscience is clear. I desire to always walk in simplicity and godly sincerity, never in fleshly wisdom. Thank you for your grace that enables me to remain simple in my approach to life even in these complex times.[5] In Jesus,[6] Amen.

References: (1) Psalms 3:7; (2) Psalms 19:7; (3) Psalms 116:6; (4) Psalms 119:130; (5) 2 Corinthians 1:12; (6) 1 Corinthians 16:24.

• SIN •

Key Scripture: "For all have sinned and fall short of the glory of God" (Rom. 3:23, NIV).

Prayer: O Sovereign Lord,[1] thank you for showing me that I need a Savior.[2] The wages of sin is death, but your free gift to me is eternal life through Jesus Christ.[3] Thank you, Father. You commended your love toward me in that while I was yet a sinner your Son died for me.[4] Now I do not have to serve sin any longer.[5] I have been set free.[6] By grace through faith I have been saved from my sin.[7] I will walk in the light with you, Lord, and the blood of Jesus Christ will continue to cleanse me from all sin.[8] In His name,[9] Amen.

References: (1) Psalms 109:21; (2) 1 John 4:14; (3) Romans 6:23; (4) Romans 5:8; (5) Romans 6:11; (6) Romans 6:17; (7) Romans 6:18; (8) 1 John 1:7; (9) 1 John 5:20.

Fewer words, less sin.

In the multitude of words there wanteth not sin:
but he that refraineth his lips is wise
(Proverbs 10:19).

• SPEECH •

Key Scripture: "Let your speech always be with grace, seasoned with salt, that you may know how you ought to answer each one" (Col. 4:6, NKJV).

Prayer: Lord God,[1] thank you for the gift of speech. Help me always to remember that in an unnecessary multitude of words sin can be found.[2] I want to follow your will by being swift to hear, slow to speak, and slow to wrath.[3] I want to be like Paul, not using excellency of speech, but simplicity[4] as I speak the truth in love.[5] Through your power, I will be able to use my speech to demonstrate your wisdom and your Spirit.[6] I choose to be sober-minded, walking in good works, gravity, and sincerity, so that my speech will always be sound.[7] Through Jesus Christ, my Lord,[8] Amen.

References: (1) Ezekiel 7:2; (2) Proverbs 10:19; (3) James 1:19; (4) 1 Corinthians 2:1; (5) Ephesians 4:15; (6) 1 Corinthians 2:6; (7) Titus 2:6-8; (8) 2 Timothy 4:22.

• SPIRITUALITY •

Key Scripture: "The mind of sinful man is death, but the mind controlled by the Spirit is life and peace" (Rom. 8:6, NIV).

Prayer: My King and my God,[1] you have blessed me with all spiritual blessings in heavenly places in Christ.[2] You are filling me with the knowledge of your will in all wisdom and spiritual understanding.[3] Therefore, I will walk worthy of you unto all pleasing, being fruitful in every good work, and increasing in my knowledge of you.[4] Thank you for strengthening me with all might, according to your glorious power, unto all patience with joyfulness.[5] Father, I thank you for enabling me to become a partaker of your spiritual inheritance with all the saints.[6] In Jesus,[7] Amen.

References: (1) Psalms 5:2; (2) Ephesians; (3) Colossians 1:9; (4) Colossians 1:10; (5) Colossians 1:11; (6) Colossians 1:12; (7) Colossians 5:23.

• STEADINESS •

Key Scripture: "So then, just as you received Christ Jesus as Lord, continue to live in him, rooted and built up in him, strengthened in the faith as you were taught, and overflowing with thankfulness" (Col. 2:6-7, NIV).

Prayer: Mighty One, God, the Lord,[1] my faith in Christ is firm.[2] You are the living God who is steadfast forever,[3] and I want to be like you. I thank you, Father, for giving me complete victory through Jesus Christ, my Lord.[4] Because of His victory in my life, I will remain steady, constant, consistent, unmoveable, always abounding in your work, Lord. I realize that my labors will never be in vain when I abide in you.[5] In Jesus,[6] Amen.

References: (1) Psalms 50:1; (2) Colossians 2:5; (3) Daniel 6:26; (4) 1 Corinthians 15:57; (5) 1 Corinthians 15:58; (6) Galatians 1:3.

You can become your strongest in your weakest moment.

But he said to me, "My grace is sufficient for you, for my power is made perfect in weakness." Therefore I will boast all the more gladly about my weaknesses, so that Christ's power may rest on me (2 Corinthians 12:9, NIV).

• STRENGTH •

Key Scripture: "The Lord is my light and my salvation; whom shall I fear? the Lord is the strength of my life; of whom shall I be afraid?" (Ps. 27:1).

Prayer: Lord, the God of hosts,[1] strengthen me according to your Word.[2] You are the God of my strength.[3] Send out your light and your truth, and let them lead me.[4] Thank you for being my refuge and strength, a very present help to me in times of trouble.[5] Because I have your strength, I will not fear.[6] I remember so well, Lord, the time when I was without strength.[7] Now, I am strong in you and in the power of your might.[8] In His name I pray,[9] Amen.

References: (1) 1 Kings 19:10; (2) Psalms 119:28; (3) Psalms 43:2; (4) Psalms 43:3; (5) Psalms 46:1; (6) Psalms 46:2; (7) Romans 5:6; (8) Ephesians 6:10; (9) John 16:24.

Temptation provokes me to look upward to God.

(John Bunyan)

Blessed is the man that endureth temptation; for when he is tried, he shall receive the crown of life, which the Lord hath promised to them that love him (James 1:12).

• TEMPTATION •

Key Scripture: "And God is faithful; he will not let you be tempted beyond what you can bear. But when you are tempted, he will also provide a way out so that you can stand up under it" (1 Cor. 10:13, NIV).

Prayer: God, my Father,[1] thank you for your Word which I will hide in my heart so as not to sin against you.[2] Jesus defeated Satan in the wilderness by standing on the promises of your Word,[3] and I will do likewise. Through your power I will endure temptation and you will give me a crown of life which you have promised to all who love you.[4] I love you, Father, with all my heart, soul, mind, and strength[5] because you first loved me.[6] In Jesus' name I pray,[7] Amen.

References: (1) 1 Corinthians 8:6; (2) Psalms 119:11; (3) Luke 4; (4) James 1:12; (5) Matthew 22:37; (6) 1 John 4:19; (7) John 16:23.

• TENDER-HEARTEDNESS •

Key Scripture: "Let all bitterness, wrath, anger, clamor, and evil speaking be put away from you, with all malice. And be kind to one another, tenderhearted, forgiving one another, just as God in Christ forgave you" (Eph. 4:31-32, NKJV).

Prayer: Heavenly Father,[1] I remember your tender mercies in my life.[2] Your lovingkindness is better than life to me.[3] I want to imitate you, Father, by being tender-hearted in all my relationships.[4] With your help, I will live a life of love, just as Christ loved me and gave himself up for me as a fragrant offering and sacrifice to you.[5] Help me to forgive others as you have forgiven me,[6] and to receive others as you have received me.[7] In Jesus' name I pray,[8] Amen.

References: (1) Luke 11:2; (2) Psalms 25:6; (3) Psalms 63:3; (4) Ephesians 5:1; (5) Ephesians 5:2; (6) Luke 11:4; (7) Romans 15:7; (8) Matthew 1:23.

• THANKSGIVING •

Key Scripture: "Amen! Praise and glory and wisdom and thanks and honor and power and strength be to our God for ever and ever. Amen!" (Rev. 7:12, NIV).

Prayer: O God,[1] I will praise your name with a song, and I will magnify you with thanksgiving.[2] It is a good thing to give thanks to you, Lord, and to sing praises to your name, O Most High.[3] I will show forth your lovingkindness in the morning and your faithfulness every night.[4] I will remain rooted and built up in Jesus Christ my Lord, being established in the faith as I have been taught, and I will always abound therein with thanksgiving.[5] In Jesus' name,[6] Amen.

References: (1) Psalms 69:1; (2) Psalms 69:30; (3) Psalms 92:1; (4) Psalms 92:2; (5) Colossians 2:7; (6) John 16:24.

• THOUGHTS •

Key Scripture: "Casting down arguments and every high thing that exalts itself against the knowledge of God, bringing every thought into captivity to the obedience of Christ" (2 Cor. 10:5, NKJV).

Prayer: God, my Father,[1] renew my mind[2] as I learn to become spiritually-minded[3] by washing in the water of your Word.[4] Your Word is alive and powerful. It is sharper than any two-edged sword as it pierces to the dividing asunder of soul and spirit and of the joints and marrow, and it is a discerner of my thoughts and intentions.[5] I want my thoughts to be like your thoughts, Lord,[6] so I will keep my mind stayed on you.[7] In Jesus' name,[8] Amen.

References: (1) Galatians 1:1; (2) Ephesians 4:23; (3) Romans 8:6; (4) Ephesians 5:26; (5) Hebrews 4:12; (6) Isaiah 55:8; (7) Isaiah 26:3; (8) Acts 2:21.

• TRUST •

Key Scripture: "Trust in the Lord with all your heart and lean not on your own understanding; in all your ways acknowledge him, and he will make your paths straight" (Prov. 3:5-6, NIV).

Prayer: O Lord,[1] trusting in you makes me happy.[2] I put my complete trust in you, and as I do so, I know you will save me and deliver me.[3] Because I trust in you I am able to rejoice, and I experience the tremendous joy that comes to all who love your name.[4] Lord, I thank you for the many blessings you have poured upon me.[5] Because I trust you, Father, I know that I will never be led into confusion.[6] Because I trust you, I now experience your perfect peace in my life.[7] In Jesus' name,[8] Amen.

References: (1) Psalms 94:1; (2) Psalms 2:12; (3) Psalms 7:1; (4) Psalms 5:11; (5) Psalms 5:12; (6) Psalms 71:1; (7) Isaiah 26:3; (8) Acts 4:12.

• TRUTH •

Key Scripture: "And you shall know the truth, and the truth shall make you free'" (John 8:32, NKJV).

Prayer: Lord,[1] lead me in your truth and teach me, for you are the God of my salvation, and I wait on you all day long.[2] All of your paths are mercy and truth when I am careful to walk in your Word.[3] Examine me, O Lord, and prove me; try my heart.[4] Your lovingkindness is before my eyes as I walk in your truth.[5] Your Son, my Lord and Savior, Jesus Christ, is the way, the truth, and the life for me, and I am able to come before you, Father, only through Him.[6] Thank you for giving me the Spirit of truth who dwells with me and within me.[7] I know He will guide me into all truth.[8] In Jesus' name,[9] Amen.

References: (1) Psalms 31:1; (2) Psalms 25:5; (3) Psalms 25:10; (4) Psalms 26:2; (5) Psalms 26:3; (6) John 14:6; (7) John 14:7; (8) John 16:13; (9) John 16:24.

• UNDERSTANDING •

Key Scripture: "Give me understanding, and I shall keep Your law; Indeed, I shall observe it with my whole heart" (Ps. 119:34, NKJV).

Prayer: O Lord,[1] please give me understanding so that I will learn all the commandments of your Word and walk in them.[2] By reading and studying your Word I get understanding.[3] Your Word is a lamp unto my feet and a light unto my path.[4] O how I love your Word; it is my meditation all day long.[5] The righteousness of your Word is everlasting, Father; therefore, I ask you to give me understanding so that I may live fully in this world.[6] In Jesus' name,[7] Amen.

References: (1) Psalms 119:33; (2) Psalms 119:73; (3) Psalms 119:104; (4) Psalms 119:105; (5) Psalms 119:97; (6) Psalms 119:144; (7) John 15:16.

• VICTORY •

Key Scripture: "And this is the victory that has overcome the world — our faith" (1 John 5:4, NKJV).

Prayer: Heavenly Father,[1] thank you for always giving me victory through Jesus Christ, my Lord.[2] When the enemy comes in like a flood, you will always raise up a standard against him.[3] Your Word will keep me from sin,[4] and I will always be victorious through faith in the name of Jesus,[5] His blood,[6] and your Word.[7] In all things you make me more than a conqueror through Christ who loved me.[8] In Jesus' name I pray,[9] Amen.

References: (1) Philippians 1:2; (2) 1 Corinthians 15:57; (3) Isaiah 59:19; (4) Psalms 119:11; (5) John 15:16; (6) Revelation 12:11; (7) Hebrews 4:12; (8) Romans 8:37; (9) John 16:24.

• WAITING •

Key Scripture: "Wait for the Lord; be strong and take heart and wait for the Lord" (Ps. 27:14, NIV).

Prayer: God, my King,[1] I find my rest in you, and the rest you give to me enables me to wait patiently for you and to keep from worry.[2] I will wait on you and keep your ways, knowing that you will enable me to inherit the land.[3] Because of your strength I will wait upon you, because I know you are my defense.[4] Through your Spirit I wait for the hope of righteousness by faith.[5] I know that the infilling of your Spirit in my life develops patience in my soul.[6] In Jesus' name,[7] Amen.

References: (1) Psalms 145:1; (2) Psalms 37:7; (3) Psalms 37:34; (4) Psalms 59:9; (5) Galatians 5:5; (6) Galatians 5:22; (7) Acts 19:17.

• WARFARE •

Key Scripture: "No weapon formed against you shall prosper" (Isa. 54:17, NKJV).

Prayer: Heavenly Father,[1] I thank you that the weapons of my warfare are not carnal but are mighty through you for the pulling down of strongholds. They enable me to cast down imaginations, arguments, and every high thing that tries to exalt itself against the knowledge of you, to bring into captivity every thought to the obedience of Christ, and to win in warfare against the enemy.[2] The weapons you give me are your Word,[3] the name of Jesus,[4] the blood of Jesus, the word of my testimony,[5] and the power of your Holy Spirit.[6] I resist the devil and he flees from me[7] because greater is He that is in me than he that is in the world.[8] In Jesus' name I pray.[9] Amen.

References: (1) Philippians 1:2; (2) 2 Corinthians 10:3-5; (3) Ephesians 6:17; (4) Mark 16:17; (5) Revelation 12:11; (6) Acts 1:8; (7) James 4:7; (8) 1 John 4:4; (9) John 15:26.

• WEAKNESS •

Key Scripture: "But he said to me, "My grace is sufficient for you, for my power is made perfect in weakness." Therefore I will boast all the more gladly about my weaknesses, so that Christ's power may rest on me" (2 Cor. 12:9, NIV).

Prayer: God, my Father,[1] your weakness is more powerful than the strength of mankind.[2] I can do all things through Christ who strengthens me.[3] You have always had mercy upon me when I've been weak.[4] Thank you, Father. You have chosen the foolish things of the world to confound the wise and mighty, and you have chosen me.[5] You have allowed Jesus Christ, your Son, to become my strength, my righteousness, my sanctification, my redemption.[6] I glory in Him.[7] In His name I pray,[8] Amen

References: (1) Galatians 1:3; (2) 1 Corinthians 1:25; (3) Philippians 4:13; (4) Psalms 6:2; (5) 1 Corinthians 1:27; (6) 1 Corinthians 1:30; (7) 1 Corinthians 1:31; (8) Revelation 19:13.

• WISDOM •

Key Scripture: "But of Him you are in Christ Jesus, who became for us wisdom from God; and righteousness and sanctification and redemption" (1 Cor. 1:30, NKJV).

Prayer: Lord God,[1] fill me with your wisdom and the knowledge of your will in all wisdom, Lord.[2] This will enable me to walk worthy of you and to please you and to be fruitful in every good work, increasing in my knowledge of you.[3] Through your wisdom, Father, I am strengthened with all might, according to your glorious power, and this gives me patience and joyfulness.[4] In Jesus' name,[5] Amen.

References: (1) Nehemiah 9:7; (2) Colossians 1:9; (3) Colossians 1:10; (4) Colossians 1:11; (5) Acts 3:16.

• WITNESSING •

Key Scripture: "But you shall receive power when the Holy Spirit has come upon you; and you shall be witnesses to Me" (Acts 1:8, NKJV).

Prayer: Father,[1] thank you for choosing me to be a disciple of Jesus Christ who will bear much fruit.[2] It is a privilege to be your ambassador.[3] Wherever I go I will share the good news about Jesus Christ,[4] because I know you want all to come to a saving knowledge of your Son.[5] You have called me to be your witness, Lord.[6] I will not be ashamed of your gospel because I know it is your power unto salvation to all who will believe.[7] In Jesus' name I pray,[8] Amen.

References: (1) Acts 1:7; (2) John 15:16; (3) 2 Corinthians 5:20; (4) Mark 16:15; (5) 2 Peter 3:9; (6) Isaiah 43:12; (7) Romans 1:16; (8) John 15:16.

• WORSHIP •

Key Scripture: "You are worthy, our Lord and God, to receive glory and honor and power, for you created all things" (Rev. 4:11, NIV).

Prayer: Lord God Almighty,[1] the hour has come when true worshipers shall worship you in spirit and in truth. You seek people who will enter into full spiritual worship in your presence, and I will be such a worshiper, Father.[2] Thank you for enabling me to serve you with gladness, and to come before you with singing.[3] You are my God, my Creator, and my Shepherd.[4] I enter your gates with thanksgiving and go into your courts with praise. I bless your name because you are good, and your mercy and truth are everlasting.[5] In Jesus' name,[6] Amen.

References: (1) Revelation 4:8; (2) John 4:23; (3) Psalms 100:2; (4) Psalms 100:3; (5) Psalms 100:4-5; (6) Acts 4:12.

• ZEAL •

Key Scripture: "... that He [Jesus] might redeem us from every lawless deed and purify for Himself His own special people, zealous for good works" (Titus 2:13-14, NKJV).

Prayer: God, my Savior,[1] your spiritual zeal has accomplished so many wonderful things in my life.[2] Indeed, your zeal causes me to become zealous of your spiritual gifts.[3] I have great zeal for you, Lord.[4] I am zealous for your Word which is very pure, and I love it so much.[5] I will put on righteousness as my breastplate and your helmet of salvation upon my head. My cloak will be the zeal you have imparted to me.[6] In Jesus' name,[7] Amen.

References: (1) Titus 1:3; (2) Isaiah 9:7; (3) 1 Corinthians 14:12; (4) 2 Kings 10:16; (5) Psalms 119:140; (6) Isaiah 59:17; (7) John 14:13.